JUNE ROTH'S

« THOUSAND CALORIE »

COOK BOOK

ARCO PUBLISHING, INC.
NEW YORK

TABLE OF CONTENTS

Revised Edition, First Printing
Published by Arco Publishing, Inc.
219 Park Avenue South, New York, N. Y. 10003

Copyright © 1967, 1975, 1979 by June Roth

Library of Congress Cataloging in Publication Data

Roth, June Spiewak.
June Roth's thousand calorie cook book.

Includes index.
1. Low-calorie diet—Recipes.   I. Title.   II. Title: Thousand calorie cook book.
RM222.2.R67 1979   641.5'635   78-10102
ISBN 0-668-04718-6

Printed in the United States of America

June Roth, creative cook and author of books about cooking, lives with her husband in an English Tudor home in suburban New Jersey. There, in her geranium pink kitchen, she evolved the menus and recipes which appear in this book.

You will find her calorie-conscious recipes as simple to prepare as they are delicious, for she has combined culinary skill with a practical philosophy of short-cut cooking.

She has a nationally syndicated column "Special Diets" and is the author of twentyfive popular cookbooks.

AN INTRODUCTION TO SLIMNESS

Are you tired of boring diets? Are you unwilling to give up a small dessert after lunch, and a slice of cake with your dinner coffee? Do you wish somebody would devise a daily menu of delicious meals that subtracts calories and yet offers you a way of eating that satisfies your need for tempting foods?

There is no magical way to eliminate calories, but there is a method of choosing a combination of lower calorie foods that are attractive and filling. Here is a four-week series of daily thousand calorie menus, that insist upon pampering you with many courses of appealing platters. Every luncheon has a little sweet dessert. Every dinner has a low-calorie cake or pie. Every menu indicates portion amounts, tantalizing garnishes to use, how to prepare unusual items, and recipes wherever necessary.

The trouble with dieting is that it has to be done by people who love to eat! There are enough dieting schemes that stress low-calorie foods in a wholesome way, but unfortunately the people who love to eat just don't stick to boring meals, however good their intentions when they start. One cannot underestimate the psychological factor in dieting.

So, what is the choice? Diet sporadically and fluctuate your weight according to your degree of will power? Or decide that while you can whittle hundreds of calories out of your daily menu, you still intend to face an interesting looking platter with appetizing food? If you have tried other methods and failed, why don't you follow this series of delicious menus that are appealing and yet add up to a mere thousand calories a day. There are no tricks involved, just the chore of counting calories removed, as you dine in the security of knowing that you are enjoying your meals and slimming at the same time.

Making up your mind to do something about excess weight is the first step. Finding a workable plan is another. Did you know that each pound of your excess weight represents 3500 calories that your body did not need? To lose that 3500 calories of stored fat, you will have to subtract that amount of food from your usual weekly menus. To lose two pounds a week, you will have to subtract 7000 calories from your regular eating habits.

A thousand calories a day does not mean a starvation diet for one who is craftily choosy about getting one's calories' worth. Figuring out the value of each food you eat is a good asset. Having someone do it for you is even better! These menus are devised to satisfy a person who likes to have several courses at each meal, and who enjoys eating. By having a thousand calorie daily menu mapped out for you, you should have no trouble keeping track of the few extras you might add each day. Don't let dieting get dreary! Keep the food colorful. Take your time when eating it, and do make up your mind to dine well while choosing low-calorie foods.

If your doctor prefers you to have several hundred more calories each day, use them to embellish the basic menus by adding skim milk to your coffee, a fruit snack, a few extra vegetables, or another slice of bread. Refer to the special Food Brand Index of Calorie Counts or the General Calorie Counts Index at the end of this book, when you wonder what you are adding to your diet.

For under a hundred calories, you may add a "Slim Shake" for a bedtime snack. Pour a glass of skim milk and two crushed ice cubes into your blender, and add instant coffee, vanilla, or ¼ cup of any fresh fruit or berries. Fill up with a refreshing, delicious Slim Shake, as a nightcap for another successful day of dieting.

Avoid substitutions wherever possible, except for the dinner dessert when you may have a 2" segment of Angel Food Cake or Sponge Cake in place of the low-calorie special dessert of the day.

If you don't enjoy your meals, you won't stay with any diet. That is why the menus included here are designed to be tasty, streamlined, filling, and portion-controlled . . . a must combination for stick-to-it dieting. Don't cheat yourself of the pleasure of dining at several courses at each meal, but do play fair and measure your portions accurately. Follow the suggestions for sprinkling and garnishing with extra flavor whenever mentioned. It adds no more calories but it does make the difference between feeding and dining!

June Roth

THOUSAND CALORIE,

FOUR WEEK

MENUS AND RECIPES

MONDAY, FIRST WEEK

BREAKFAST

½ Pink Grapefruit, topped with
1 teaspoon dietetic Black Raspberry Jelly
*Cheese Omelet
Coffee or Tea

LUNCHEON

*Open-faced Broiled Hamburger
Broiled: ½ Tomato, sprinkled with
oregano and Accent, and
½ Peach, rinsed if canned in syrup, and
2 large Mushroom Caps, open side up
Dessert: Raspberry D-Zerta Gelatin
Coffee or Tea

BIRDS EYE MIXED FRUIT

DINNER

1 cup Bouillon, garnished with
several croutons
*Fillet of Flounder with Sour Cream Sauce
½ cup cooked Chopped Spinach
Baked Potato, medium sized, with
1 teaspoon butter, and
1 teaspoon chopped chives
Salad: Shredded Lettuce
½ Cucumber, sliced
*Wine Vinegar Dressing
*Dessert: Mixed Fruit Ambrosia
Coffee or Tea

CHEESE OMELET

1 egg, beaten	1 slice American cheese

Pour one beaten egg into a heated Teflon skillet, cover with one slice of American cheese when egg is partially set and cover pan for several minutes. Serve immediately.

OPEN-FACED BROILED HAMBURGER

⅛ pound lean ground beef	Accent Onion salt
1 slice protein bread	

Spread lean ground beef over slice of protein bread. Sprinkle with Accent and onion salt. Broil for three minutes, or until done to your taste.

FILLET OF FLOUNDER WITH SOUR CREAM SAUCE

1 pound fillet of flounder	Paprika
1 lemon	2 tablespoons dried onion flakes
2 tablespoons sour cream	1 tablespoon dried parsley flakes

Arrange fillets on a broiler pan. Sprinkle with lemon juice. Spread with sour cream. Sprinkle with paprika, onion flakes, and parsley. Broil ten minutes. Serves 2.

WINE VINEGAR DRESSING

2 ounces wine vinegar	½ teaspoon sugar Dash of salt
1 ounce water	and pepper

Combine in a glass, mix vigorously and pour over salad.

MIXED FRUIT AMBROSIA

1 package (12 ounce) frozen mixed fruit	¼ cup flaked coconut

Remove block of fruit from carton. Place in bowl and sprinkle coconut over fruit. Let stand at room temperature until just thawed (about 2½ hours). Mix gently. Makes 4 servings.

TUESDAY
FIRST WEEK

BREAKFAST
½ cup Orange and Grapefruit segments,
fresh or canned water-pack
1 slice Raisin Toast, topped with
1 Poached Egg
Coffee or Tea

LUNCHEON
½ cup Tomato Juice
*Broiled Shrimp
½ cup Broccoli, seasoned with lemon wedge
½ cup Tiny Whole Carrots, canned
Dessert: ½ Peach, molded in
½ cup Lemon D-Zerta Gelatin
Coffee or Tea

DINNER
1 cup Vegetable Soup
¼ pound Broiled Calves' Liver, garnished
with several canned French Fried
Onion Rings
½ cup String Beans, garnished with a pinch
of Slivered Almonds
½ cup Spaghetti, cooked and mixed with
¼ cup canned Tomato Puree
*Salad: Pickled Cucumbers
*Dessert: Coffee Pudding
Coffee or Tea

BROILED SHRIMP

For each serving:

3 ounces cleaned shrimp	1 crushed clove garlic
1 tablespoon olive oil	1 teaspoon chopped parsley

Roll the raw cleaned peeled shrimp in a
sauce of the combined olive oil, garlic,
and parsley. Broil until pink (about five
minutes).

PICKLED CUCUMBERS

1 cucumber, sliced paper thin	¼ teaspoon Sucaryl Solution
1 onion, sliced paper thin	½ teaspoon salt Pepper
½ cup vinegar	¼ cup water

Mix cucumber and onion slices in a
small deep bowl. Combine the vinegar,
Sucaryl Solution, salt, a dash of pepper,
and the water in a glass, mixing vigorously. Pour over cucumber slices and
marinate for several hours, in the refrigerator.

COFFEE PUDDING

2 tablespoons instant coffee	1½ tablespoons Sucaryl Solution
¼ teaspoon salt	2 eggs, slightly beaten
⅓ cup flour	1 teaspoon vanilla
2 cups skim milk, scalded	

Combine coffee, salt and flour in the top
of a double boiler, add scalded milk
slowly to make a smooth sauce. Add
Sucaryl and eggs, stirring thoroughly.
Cook over hot water, stirring until thick.
Cool. Add vanilla and pour into dessert
dishes. Garnish with dietetic whipped
topping. Serves 5.

PHOTOGRAPH: ABBOTT LABORATORIES

WEDNESDAY
FIRST WEEK

BREAKFAST
Fresh Orange Slices (½ an orange)
*Cottage Cheese and Egg Blintz
1 slice Whole Wheat Toast
Coffee or Tea

LUNCHEON
½ cup Tomato Juice
Salmon Salad: 3¾-ounce can of Salmon
on bed of Lettuce, garnished with
quartered medium Tomato,
½ cup Asparagus Spears,
1 quartered fresh or water-pack Pear
Dessert: Lime D-Zerta Gelatin
Coffee or Tea

DINNER
1 cup Clam Chowder, Manhattan style
*Chicken Mandarin
½ cup cooked Broccoli, seasoned
with Lemon Wedge
½ cup Minute Rice, cooked in broth
instead of water
Salad: Shredded Lettuce and scraped
"pennies" of Carrots
Dietetic French Dressing
Dessert: Thin slice Sponge Cake
Coffee or Tea

COTTAGE CHEESE AND EGG BLINTZ

1 egg, beaten	2 tablespoons cottage cheese

Lightly butter a small skillet. Heat on a low flame. Pour in beaten egg. Cover a moment until set. Flip onto plate, place two tablespoons of cottage cheese along one edge and roll up.

CHICKEN MANDARIN

1 broiler, about 3 pounds	⅛ teaspoon rosemary
1 tablespoon cornstarch	1 can (small) mandarin oranges
⅛ teaspoon marjoram	

Quarter chicken and broil on both sides for twenty minutes. Meanwhile, combine the cornstarch with the marjoram and rosemary in a small saucepan. Add the liquid from the mandarin oranges and mix until smooth. Cook and stir until sauce is thick. Add orange slices. Pour over broiled chicken. Serves 4.

PHOTOGRAPH: CANNED SALMON INSTITUTE

11

THURSDAY FIRST WEEK

BREAKFAST

½ cup Grapefruit Sections, fresh or
canned water-pack, garnished with
1 tablespoon crushed pineapple (canned)
*Baked Egg in English Muffin
Coffee or Tea

LUNCHEON

1 cup Tomato Bouillon: Blend ½ cup
Bouillon with ½ cup Tomato Juice; heat
Tuna Salad Platter: For each serving,
arrange half a 7-ounce can of drained Tuna
on bed of Lettuce, garnish with 1
teaspoon salad dressing and chopped
chives; add Celery and Carrot Sticks
on the side
Dessert: ½ cup canned water-pack
Apricots, garnished with
1 teaspoon Seedless Raisins
Coffee or Tea

DINNER

1 cup canned Onion Soup, garnished with
1 teaspoon grated Parmesan Cheese
*Veal Marsala
*Zucchini Jumble
½ cup Stewed Tomatoes, with a
pinch of oregano
Salad: Wedge of lettuce, with a strip of
pimento and dash of Wine Vinegar
*Chocolate/Vanilla Parfait Pudding
Coffee or Tea

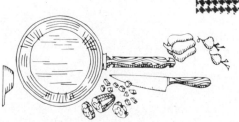

BAKED EGG IN ENGLISH MUFFIN

1 egg   ½ English muffin

Scoop out soft part of one half an
English muffin, discard. Fill muffin center with a raw egg. Bake in a 400 degree
oven for fifteen minutes, or until set to
taste.

VEAL MARSALA

1 pound veal, thinly   ½ cup Marsala
  sliced   wine
¼ cup flour   Salt
2 tablespoons   Pepper
  butter

Lightly dredge the thinly sliced veal in
the flour. Brown in butter in a heavy
skillet. Turn. Add Marsala wine, season
with salt and pepper. Cover pan and
simmer over low heat for five minutes.
Serves 4.

ZUCCHINI JUMBLE

2 zucchini   2 tablespoons
10 mushrooms   olive oil
2 stalks celery

Cut zucchini into ½-inch slices. Slice
mushrooms and celery. Sauté in olive
oil, stirring, for five minutes. Serves 4.

CHOCOLATE/VANILLA PARFAIT PUDDING

1 envelope (4-   1 envelope (4-
  serving size) low-   serving size) low-
  calorie chocolate   calorie vanilla
  pudding (D-Zerta)   pudding (D-Zerta)
  prepared with   prepared with
  nonfat milk.   nonfat milk.

Prepare separately chocolate and vanilla puddings as directed on packages.
Alternately layer cooled puddings in
parfait glasses, using about ¼ cup
each flavor per glass, beginning and
ending with the chocolate pudding, and
reserving a small amount of vanilla
pudding for garnish. Makes 8 parfaits.

WEIGHT LOSS CHART

WEIGHT 1 2 3 4 5 6 7 8 9 10

WEEK

2nd WEEK

3 WEEK

4 WEEK

FRIDAY
FIRST WEEK

BREAKFAST
½ sliced fresh Orange
1 fried Egg on
1 ounce lean trimmed slice of Boiled Ham
Coffee or Tea

LUNCHEON
1 cup Vegetable Soup
Cottage Cheese Fruit Salad: On a bed of
Shredded Lettuce, place ⅔ cup
Cottage Cheese,
add 1 cup assorted water-pack fruits
1 slice Whole Wheat Toast,
1 teaspoon butter
Dessert: Orange D-Zerta Gelatin
Coffee or Tea

DINNER
1 cup Bouillon, thin lemon slice floating
*Shrimp Parmesan
½ cup cooked Green Noodles,
1 teaspoon butter
½ cup sliced cooked Carrots
½ Broiled Tomato, sprinkled with
oregano and Accent
*Dessert: Lemon Pudding Cake
Coffee or Tea

SHRIMP PARMESAN

Frozen breaded shrimp
Mozzarella cheese

Grated Parmesan cheese

Arrange frozen breaded shrimp on a broiling pan, allowing eight per serving. Cover with thin slices of Mozzarella cheese and sprinkle with grated Parmesan cheese. Broil five minutes.

LEMON PUDDING CAKE

½ cup flour
½ teaspoon baking powder
2 eggs, separated
2 teaspoons grated lemon rind
¼ cup fresh lemon juice

1½ cups skim milk
2 teaspoons Adolph's Granulated Sugar Substitute

Sift flour and baking powder. Beat egg yolks until lemon-colored; add rest of ingredients; beat thoroughly. Add flour mixture, beat until smooth. Beat egg whites until stiff, fold into egg yolk mixture. Pour into a 1-quart greased baking dish. Set in pan of hot water. Bake at 350° for 30 minutes. Cool. Pudding will separate into cake layer and sauce layer. Serves 6.

PHOTOGRAPH: ADOLPH'S LTD.

15

SATURDAY
FIRST WEEK

BREAKFAST
½ cup Orange Juice
1 cup Puffed Rice
½ cup Skim Milk
Coffee or Tea

LUNCHEON
½ cup V-8 Juice, Lime Wedge
*Egg Lorraine
Dessert: ½ cup sliced Peaches,
water-packed or rinsed
Coffee or Tea

DINNER
*Broiled Half Grapefruit
Sliced Steak, 4-ounce serving,
well trimmed of fat
* ½ Acorn Squash, with Applesauce Filling
½ cup String Beans
½ cup Sliced Carrots
Salad: Shredded Bib Lettuce,
3 Cherry Tomatoes
Dash of Wine Vinegar
Dessert: 1 Thin Slice Sponge Cake,
2″ segment
Coffee or Tea

EGG LORRAINE

1 egg, beaten	2 slices bacon,
½ onion, chopped	crisply cooked
1 ounce Swiss	
cheese, chopped	

To beaten egg, add chopped onion, chopped Swiss cheese and crumbled slices of bacon. Pour into lightly greased skillet and cook until set to your taste.

BROILED HALF GRAPEFRUIT

½ grapefruit	Dash of cinnamon
1 teaspoon brown	
sugar	

Sprinkle cut side of grapefruit with brown sugar and cinnamon. Broil ten minutes, or until lightly browned.

ACORN SQUASH, APPLESAUCE FILLING

2 acorn squash	2 teaspoons lemon
⅔ cup applesauce,	juice
unsweetened	2 tablespoons
¼ teaspoon	raisins
Sucaryl Solution	2 teaspoons butter

Scrub, halve, and remove seeds from squash. Mix applesauce, Sucaryl, lemon juice and raisins together, and fill squash halves. Dot with butter. Place in a flat baking dish, adding water to the bottom of dish. Cover and bake in 400° oven for 20 minutes. Remove cover and bake 15 minutes more, or until tender. Serves 4.

17

SUNDAY
FIRST WEEK

BREAKFAST
½ cup Pineapple Juice
*Salami Omelet
Coffee or Tea

LUNCHEON
1 cup Bouillon, with several croutons
1 Grilled Frankfurter
1 cup Sauerkraut w. celery seed
1 large Dill Pickle
Dessert: ½ cup fresh raw Strawberries,
sprinkled with 1 teaspoon powdered sugar
Coffee or Tea

DINNER
½ cup Tomato Juice
* ½ Roasted Rock Cornish Hen
1 Boiled Potato, with 1 teaspoon butter and
1 teaspoon parsley
6 Asparagus Spears
½ cup Beets
Salad: Shredded Lettuce, 1 Artichoke Heart,
1 strip Pimento
Dietetic Italian style dressing
*Dessert: Coffee Crème
Coffee or Tea

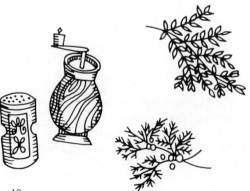

SALAMI OMELET

1 egg, beaten	1 thin slice salami, diced

Pour egg into a lightly greased skillet. Sprinkle with diced salami slice. Cook until set. Serve immediately.

ROASTED ROCK CORNISH HEN

2 Rock Cornish hens	1 tablespoon dietetic orange marmalade
1 tablespoon melted butter	

Brush hens with melted butter and roast in 400° oven for about forty-five minutes. Brush marmalade over the tops of hens and continue roasting for fifteen minutes more. Serves 4.

COFFEE CRÈME

1 cup non-dairy Pream	Dash of salt
1 envelope unflavored gelatin	3 eggs, separated
	1 tablespoon liquid Sucaryl
2 tablespoons instant coffee	2 cups boiling water
	1 teaspoon vanilla

In top of double boiler, combine Pream, gelatin, instant coffee and salt. Beat egg yolks and add to mixture with Sucaryl and boiling water. Cook over hot water, stirring constantly until gelatin dissolves and mixture coats a silver spoon. Remove from heat; add vanilla; chill until mixture just begins to thicken. Beat egg whites until soft peaks form; fold into gelatin mixture; chill until mixture mounds from spoon. Spoon into dessert dish and garnish with low-calorie whipped topping. Serves 6.

PHOTOGRAPH: SWIFT & COMPANY

MONDAY
SECOND WEEK

BREAKFAST
½ Grapefruit
Slice of White Enriched Toast, topped with
1 slice of American Cheese
Coffee or Tea

LUNCHEON
*Red Caviar Omelet
½ sliced Tomato
½ cup Spinach
*Dessert: Ginger Pears
Coffee or Tea

DINNER
½ Cantaloupe
*Meat Loaf Ring, 4-ounce slice
*1 Giant Baked Mushroom
½ cup Canned Corn/Frenched
Green Beans
Salad: Shredded Lettuce, ½ sliced
Cucumber, Dietetic Dressing
Dessert: 1 slice Angel Food Cake
Coffee or Tea

RED CAVIAR OMELET

1 egg, beaten	1 teaspoon chopped
1 tablespoon sour	chives
cream	
1 tablespoon red	
caviar	

Pour beaten egg into lightly buttered skillet. Cook until set. Flip onto plate and cover one side with sour cream, topped with red caviar. Sprinkle with chopped chives. Cover with other side of omelet. Serve immediately.

GINGER PEARS

⅛ teaspoon ginger	2 pear halves
2 tablespoons	
water-pack pear	
juice	

Add ginger to pear juice in small saucepan and heat for several minutes. Add pear halves and cover for fifteen minutes, with heat turned off. Serve warm. Makes 1 serving.

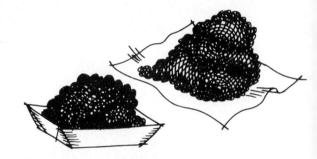

MEAT LOAF RING

¾ cup chopped	½ teaspoon basil
onion	1 teaspoon salt
1 tablespoon butter	Dash pepper
1 egg, beaten	2 cups canned
1 cup prepared	applesauce,
seasoned dry	unsweetened
bread crumbs	2 pounds ground
½ teaspoon	chuck beef
oregano	

Sauté onion in butter until delicate brown. Combine egg, seasoned crumbs, oregano, basil, salt, pepper and applesauce; mix thoroughly. Add meat and browned onion; blend well. Put meat in a greased 1½-quart ring mold and bake in a 375° oven for 60 minutes. Serves 8.

GIANT BAKED MUSHROOM

1 giant mushroom	3 cocktail onions
1 tablespoon bread	
crumbs, seasoned	

Chop mushroom stem, combine with bread crumbs. Place cocktail onions in open-side-up cavity of mushroom and spoon crumbs around them. Bake for twenty minutes in 375° oven.

TUESDAY
SECOND WEEK

BREAKFAST
½ sliced Orange
1 cup cooked Oatmeal, mixed with
½ cup Skim Milk
Coffee or Tea

LUNCHEON
*Chef's Salad
Dessert: ½ cup Peach Slices, water-pack
or rinsed regular pack
Coffee or Tea

DINNER
1 cup Clam Chowder, Manhattan Style
*Veal and Peppers
* ½ cup Rickshaw Beans
Salad: Lettuce, Raw Spinach,
with a dash of Wine Vinegar
Dessert: 2 Dietetic Vanilla Cookies, spread
with 1 teaspoon Dietetic Raspberry Jam
Coffee or Tea

CHEF'S SALAD

½ small head of lettuce, torn up
¼ cup Swiss cheese, diced
¼ cup chicken or ham, diced
¼ cup grated carrot
½ sliced tomato

Toss together and drizzle with dietetic French dressing.

VEAL AND PEPPERS

1 sliced onion
1 clove garlic
2 tablespoons olive oil
2 green peppers, seeded and cubed
1 pound veal, cubed
1 can whole tomatoes
1 small can tomato paste
½ teaspoon salt
¼ teaspoon pepper

Brown onion and garlic in olive oil. Add cubed green peppers and sauté until soft. Push aside and add cubed veal, browning lightly. Add whole tomatoes, tomato paste, salt and pepper. Simmer, covered, until tender. Serves 4.

RICKSHAW BEANS

1 9-oz. package diagonal-cut green beans frozen in butter sauce
½ cup precooked rice, measure cooked not raw
1 2½-oz. jar sliced drained mushrooms
1 teaspoon soy sauce

Cook beans and rice separately. Mix together with mushrooms and soy sauce. Serves 4.

WEDNESDAY SECOND WEEK

BREAKFAST

½ cup Grapefruit Juice, unsweetened
1 Soft Boiled Egg
1 slice Raisin Toast
1 teaspoon Dietetic Grape Jelly
Coffee or Tea

LUNCHEON

½ cup Pineapple Juice
3 ounces Lean Hamburger
½ cup Cole Slaw
1 large Pickle
Dessert: ½ cup unsweetened Applesauce,
dash of cinnamon and grated lemon peel
Coffee or Tea

DINNER

1 cup Tomato Bouillon: Heat ½ cup
Tomato Juice with ½ cup Bouillon
*Stuffed Flounder Florentine
½ cup Macaroni, tossed with
1 tablespoon Cheese Whiz
½ cup Italian Sliced Beans
*Salad: Spiced Beet Ring
*Dessert: Pineapple Whip
Coffee or Tea

STUFFED FLOUNDER FLORENTINE

1 package frozen chopped spinach	1 pound flounder fillets
1 tablespoon dried onion flakes	1 teaspoon butter Paprika
¼ teaspoon salt Dash of nutmeg	Salt

Sauce:

1 bouillon cube	1 tablespoon chopped parsley
½ cup water	
1 tablespoon onion flakes	1 teaspoon Gravy Master

Cook chopped spinach with onion flakes
and salt. Drain and season with nutmeg.

Spread on large fillets and roll up. Arrange fillets in a flat baking dish. Dot with butter and sprinkle with paprika and salt. Simmer bouillon cube in ½ cup water. When dissolved, add onion flakes, parsley, and Gravy Master; simmer for five minutes. Spoon over fillets and bake for twenty minutes in 350° oven. Serves 3.

SPICED BEET RING

1 16-oz can french style beets	¼ teaspoon cinnamon
1 package Lemon D-Zerta Gelatin	⅛ teaspoon ground cloves
¼ cup vinegar	

Drain liquid from beets, add water to make 1¾ cups. Boil, then stir in gelatin until dissolved. Add vinegar and spices. Add beets. Fill ring mold and chill. Serves 4.

PINEAPPLE WHIP

2 tablespoons unflavored gelatin	4 teaspoons Sucaryl Solution
3½ cups unsweetened pineapple juice	¼ teaspoon salt
	2 teaspoons grated lemon rind

In a small mixer bowl, soften gelatin in ½ cup of the pineapple juice. Heat remaining juice; add to gelatin, stirring to dissolve. Add Sucaryl, salt and lemon rind. Chill until mixture begins to thicken. Beat on high speed of mixer until fluffy and double in volume. Chill a few minutes until mixture mounds from spoon; spoon into 6 sherbet glasses. Chill until set. Serves 6.

THURSDAY SECOND WEEK

BREAKFAST

½ cup Orange & Grapefruit Segments,
canned water-pack
*1 slice French Toast
Coffee or Tea

LUNCHEON

1 cup Bouillon, with several croutons
*Salmon Surprise Salad
Dessert: Cherry D-Zerta Gelatin
Coffee or Tea

DINNER

½ cup Tomato Juice
*Brisket Pot Roast, two average slices
½ cup Sweet & Sour Red Cabbage, canned
*4 tiny Roasted Potatoes
Salad: Shredded Lettuce
Grated Raw Carrot
Italian-style Dietetic Dressing
*Dessert: ½ cup Orange Sherbet
Coffee or Tea

FRENCH TOAST

1 egg, beaten	2 slices white bread
1 tablespoon milk	½ teaspoon sugar

Beat milk into egg, dip in slices of bread one at a time. Brown soaked bread on a lightly buttered griddle. Turn and brown other side. Sprinkle with sugar. Serves 2.

SALMON SURPRISE SALAD

1 3¾-ounce can salmon	1 teaspoon chopped walnuts
¼ cup chopped celery	1 tablespoon mayonnaise-type salad dressing
1 teaspoon dried parsley	

Combine salmon with the chopped celery, parsley, chopped walnuts and salad dressing. Arrange on bed of lettuce. Serves 1.

BRISKET POT ROAST

3-pound cut of fresh brisket, lean	Paprika
1 package Lipton's Onion Soup Mix	

Place brisket in a small roasting pan. Sprinkle soup mix over top. Sprinkle paprika over all. Add a cup of water to the bottom of pan and cover with foil. Roast in 350° oven for two hours, removing foil the last half hour of cooking. Add water if necessary to produce more gravy.

TINY ROASTED POTATOES

Add 1 drained can of tiny whole potatoes to the brisket pot roast when you remove the foil. Roll in gravy and dash paprika over the potatoes. Roast for half hour with the brisket.

ORANGE SHERBET

¾ cup water	1 6-ounce can frozen orange juice (undiluted)
¾ cup sugar	
½ cup water	
1 tablespoon lemon juice	2 egg whites, beaten stiff, not dry
1 teaspoon almond flavoring	
½ cup non-fat dry milk solids	

Blend ¾ cup water and sugar together in a heavy pan. Stir over moderate heat until sugar dissolves. Bring to a boil without stirring, reduce heat and simmer 10 minutes. Meanwhile, place ½ cup water, lemon juice and almond flavoring in a mixing bowl. Sprinkle non-fat dry milk solids over the surface and beat until mixture is thick and fluffy. Blend in undiluted frozen orange juice. Divide mixture into two ice cube trays, and place in freezing compartment of refrigerator with dial set at fast freezing. When mixture is partially frozen, remove and break up with a fork. Beat with rotary beater, then fold in stiffly beaten egg whites. Return to freezing compartment until frozen firmly. Serves 12.

FRIDAY
SECOND WEEK

BREAKFAST
½ cup Pineapple Juice
1 Egg, scrambled
Coffee or Tea

LUNCHEON
½ cup Apple Juice
Vegetable Platter: ½ cup Cauliflower with
1 teaspoon grated Parmesan Cheese,
½ cup Spinach, dash of nutmeg;
½ cup Beets, grated orange peel;
½ broiled Tomato with dash of oregano;
½ cup Peas
1 slice Rye Bread, spread with
1 tablespoon Cottage Cheese
Dessert: 2 Peach Halves, water-pack
Coffee or Tea

DINNER
½ cup Dietetic Fruit Salad, covered with
¼ cup low-calorie Ginger Ale
*Shish-Ka-Bob
1 Corn on the Cob with
1 teaspoon butter
6 Asparagus Spears
Salad: Lettuce Wedge, 3 Cherry Tomatoes,
Dietetic Dressing
*Dessert: Strawberry Shortcake
Coffee or Tea

SHISH-KA-BOB

2 pounds lean lamb chunks	Salt
2 green peppers, seeded and cubed	Pepper
	Garlic salt (optional)
24 mushroom caps	

Skewer alternate chunks of lamb, green pepper and whole mushroom caps. Season with salt, pepper, and garlic salt. Broil for about 15 minutes. Serves 6.

STRAWBERRY SHORTCAKE

Biscuit-Type Shortcake:	3 tablespoons butter
1 cup sifted flour	1 egg
1½ teaspoons baking powder	¾ teaspoon Sucaryl Solution
Pinch of salt	¼ cup skim milk

Preheat oven to 450°. Combine flour, baking powder and salt. Cut in butter until of consistency of coarse meal. Combine remaining ingredients; stir into flour mixture. Knead gently about 10 times. Roll ¼ inch thick on lightly floured board. Cut into six 3-inch circles. Place on ungreased baking sheet; bake 12 to 15 minutes. Cool.

Strawberry Sauce:	2 tablespoons Sucaryl Solution
4 cups hulled strawberries	2 tablespoons water

Crush 1 cup of the strawberries; add Sucaryl and water. Pour over remaining whole berries and chill. Split biscuits and fill with sauce; top with remaining sauce. If desired, garnish with low-calorie whipped topping. Serves 6.

PHOTOGRAPH: ADOLPH'S LTD.

SATURDAY
SECOND WEEK

BREAKFAST
½ cup Apple Juice
1 cup cooked Cream of Wheat, with
1 teaspoon Raisins and a
Dash of Cinnamon
½ cup Skim Milk
Coffee or Tea

LUNCHEON
1 cup canned Tomato Soup using
water instead of milk
*Chicken Liver Omelet
2 Spiced Apple Rings
(dietetic canned variety)
Dessert: Lemon D-Zerta Gelatin
Coffee or Tea

DINNER
½ Grapefruit
Steak, broiled, trimmed lean, 4" x 3" x ¾"
Baked Potato, small, with
1 teaspoon Sour Cream and
Chopped Chives
½ cup Whole String Beans
½ cup Tiny Whole Carrots, heated
with a pinch of dill
Salad: ½ cup Cole Slaw
*Dessert: French Pear Tart
Coffee or Tea

PHOTO: ADOLPHS LTD.

CHICKEN LIVER OMELET

2 cut-up chicken livers	1 egg, beaten
½ cup bouillon	1 tablespoon milk
1 teaspoon grated onion	

Simmer chicken livers in the bouillon, with grated onion, over low heat for about ten minutes. Then, pour beaten egg mixed with milk into a lightly buttered skillet, cooking until set. Flip onto plate and fill with cooked chicken livers, covering one side of omelet and folding other side over. Serve immediately.

FRENCH PEAR TART

Pastry for single
crust
½ cup water
2 tablespoons liquid
Sucaryl
1 tablespoon lemon
juice
8 pears, pared,
cored and sliced
into sixths

1 8-ounce jar
Sucaryl-sweet-
ened apricot
preserves
Nutmeg

Roll pastry to fit a 12-inch tart pan. Bake in 425° oven for 12 minutes or until golden brown; remove from oven and cool. Combine water, Sucaryl and lemon juice in a saucepan; add pear slices, a few at a time, and poach about 5 minutes, or until tender. Cool slightly, drain and save ¼ cup of the liquid. Arrange pear slices, spoke fashion, in tart shell. In saucepan, combine apricot preserves and reserved liquid; heat until bubbly. Force through a sieve, then spoon over pear slices to glaze. Sprinkle with nutmeg. Chill until ready to serve. Makes 12 servings.

SUNDAY SECOND WEEK

BREAKFAST

½ sliced Orange
1 Soft Boiled Egg
1 Corn Toastie, with
1 teaspoon Butter
Coffee or Tea

LUNCHEON

½ cup V-8 Juice, lime wedge
*Salmon Loaf Milanese
¼ cup Pickled sliced Beets
Dessert: Orange D-Zerta
Coffee or Tea

DINNER

*Tomato Clam Soup
*Chicken & Artichokes
½ cup Broad Noodles, cooked
2 stalks Broccoli, cooked
Salad: Wedge of Lettuce,
Italian Dietetic Dressing
*Dessert: Peach Melba Sundae
Coffee or Tea

PHOTOGRAPH: CANNED SALMON INSTITUTE

SALMON LOAF MILANESE

2 large lemons
1-pound can salmon, including liquid from can
2 cups soda cracker crumbs
¼ teaspoon pepper
½ teaspoon salt
1 teaspoon thyme
3 eggs, lightly beaten
Parsley

Pare the yellow rind from the lemon and, with scissors, cut into slivers. Flake the salmon into a bowl and add liquid from the can, the lemon rind slivers and the juice from the lemon. Add remaining ingredients and mix well. Spoon mixture into a quart loaf pan and bake in preheated 350° oven for 30 minutes. Serve hot or cold, garnished with lemon slices and sprays of parsley. Serves 5.

TOMATO CLAM SOUP

¾ cup tomato juice
¼ cup clam juice
½ teaspoon lemon juice

Combine the juices in a small saucepan, and heat through.

CHICKEN & ARTICHOKES

8 chicken thighs
¾ cup broth
¾ cup sherry
1 package frozen artichoke hearts
1 sliced onion
½ sliced green pepper
½ teaspoon salt

Broil chicken thighs for 5 minutes on each side. Combine the broth, sherry, artichoke hearts, onion, green pepper and salt in a saucepan. Cover and cook for fifteen minutes. Arrange chicken on noodles and pour sauce over. Serves 4.

PEACH MELBA SUNDAE

½ peach, water-pack or rinsed regular pack
¼ cup vanilla ice cream
1 tablespoon dietetic raspberry jam

Place half of peach in the bottom of a dessert dish. Top with a scoop of vanilla ice cream. Pour dietetic raspberry jam on top.

MONDAY
THIRD WEEK

BREAKFAST
½ Cantaloupe
1 cup Puffed Wheat
½ cup Skim Milk
½ medium Sliced Banana
Coffee or Tea

LUNCHEON
½ cup Pineapple Juice
*Egg Florentine
1 slice Whole Wheat Bread, spread with
2 tablespoons Cottage Cheese, and a
dash of Cinnamon
Dessert: ½ cup Mandarin Oranges,
water-pack
Coffee or Tea

DINNER
1 cup Vegetable Soup
*Hamburger/Bacon Patty
½ cup Mashed Potatoes
½ cup Diced Carrots, cooked
*Salad: Gourmet Green Bean Salad
*Dessert: Strawberry Dream
Coffee or Tea

PHOTOGRAPH: S & W

34

EGG FLORENTINE

1 cup chopped cooked spinach	1 egg Dash of paprika

Fill 1 small baking dish with cooked spinach, making a depression in the center large enough to hold 1 raw egg. Bake for 10 minutes at 350°, or until firm to your taste.

HAMBURGER/BACON PATTY

4 ounces lean ground round beef 1 slice lean bacon	1 teaspoon grated dried onion flakes

Form beef into a thick patty. Wrap the slice of lean bacon around the rim. Sprinkle top with onion flakes. Broil on both sides.

GOURMET GREEN BEAN SALAD

1 16-ounce can cut green beans, drained 1 medium size onion, sliced	1 grapefruit, peeled and sectioned 1 tablespoon crumbled blue cheese

Combine in a bowl.

French Dressing: 2 tablespoons vinegar 2 tablespoons oil 1/4 teaspoon salt	1/4 teaspon paprika 1/4 teaspoon dry mustard Dash of pepper

Shake well together and pour over green bean mixture. Serves 4.

STRAWBERRY DREAM

1 cup fresh strawberries	4 tablespoons Dream Whip, dietetic whipped topping

Slice berries, and fold into Dream Whip Topping. Spoon all into a tall parfait glass. Top with one whole strawberry. Makes 1 serving.

TUESDAY
THIRD WEEK

BREAKFAST
½ Grapefruit, garnished with
1 teaspoon Dietetic Blueberry Jam
*Framed Egg
Coffee or Tea

LUNCHEON
1 cup Clam Chowder, Manhattan Style
*Cottage Cheese/Vegetable Platter
1 slice Protein Bread, with
1 teaspoon Butter
Dessert: 2 Peach Halves,
water-pack or rinsed
Coffee or Tea

DINNER
Shrimp Cocktail: 4 cooked and peeled
Shrimp, with 1 tablespoon
prepared Cocktail Sauce
*Leg of Lamb au Café
1 Boiled Potato, small
½ cup Italian Green Beans
Side Dish: ½ cup Stewed Tomatoes,
with pinch of basil
*Dessert: Prune Fluff
Coffee or Tea

FRAMED EGG
1 slice white toast   1 egg

Tear out circle in center of toast, place frame on a lightly buttered griddle and break an egg into the center. Cover and fry to your taste.

COTTAGE CHEESE/VEGETABLE PLATTER

Large lettuce cup	1 teaspoon chopped
1 large tomato	chives
¼ cup cottage	6 asparagus spears
cheese	½ slice raw
1 teaspoon sour	cucumber
cream	

On lettuce cup, place the tomato, scored into wedges almost all the way through. Fill center with cottage cheese, top with sour cream and chives. Garnish the side of platter with asparagus spears and sliced cucumber.

LEG OF LAMB AU CAFÉ

1 leg of lamb	1 cup double
Salt	strength black
Pepper	coffee

Season lamb with salt and pepper. Pour black coffee over lamb, and roast in 400° oven until done to your liking.

PRUNE FLUFF

1 5-ounce jar	1 teaspoon
strained prunes	unflavored
1½ teaspoons	gelatin
Sucaryl Solution	1 tablespoon cold
1 teaspoon vanilla	water
1 teaspoon lemon	2 egg whites
juice	
1 teaspoon grated	
lemon rind	

Blend prunes, Sucaryl, vanilla, lemon juice and rind together. Soften gelatin in cold water, then dissolve over hot water in a double boiler. Beat egg whites until frothy, add gelatin and beat very stiff. Fold into prune mixture and pile lightly into dessert glasses. Chill. If desired, top with low-calorie whipped topping. Garnish with walnut half. Serves 4.

PHOTOGRAPH: ABBOTT LABORATORIES

WEDNESDAY THIRD WEEK

BREAKFAST
½ cup Orange Juice
1 slice Protein Bread Toast, topped with
1 slice of American Cheese (the heat
of the toast should melt the cheese slightly)
Coffee or Tea

LUNCHEON
½ cup Tomato Juice, Lemon Wedge
1 Grilled Frankfurter
½ cup Cole Slaw
1 large Dill Pickle
*Dessert: Baked Apple
Coffee or Tea

DINNER
*1 cup Spinach Soup
London Broil (3 thin slices of
broiled flank steak)
2 Giant Broiled Mushroom Caps
½ cup Peas
Salad: Sliced Cucumbers and Tomatoes,
with a dash of Wine Vinegar
*Dessert: Lemon-Rice Ring
Coffee or Tea

BAKED APPLE

Apple, medium size   1 tablespoon
                             dietetic raspberry
                             jelly

Wash the apples, and pare the skins
down ¼ from the top. Core and fill
cavity with dietetic raspberry jelly. Wrap
each apple loosely in foil and place on
a baking sheet. Bake in 400° oven for
35 minutes. Cool and serve.

SPINACH SOUP

1 package frozen chopped spinach, thawed	¼ teaspoon pepper
	2 cups bouillon
	1 teaspoon flour, heaping
1 slice onion, small	
1 bay leaf	½ cup skim milk
½ teaspoon salt	1 egg yolk

Combine the spinach, onion, bay leaf,
salt, pepper and bouillon in a small
saucepan and simmer for fifteen minutes. Remove bay leaf. Blend mixture
in electric blender, or force through
sieve. Mix the flour with milk until
smooth. Stir into spinach soup over low
heat, and simmer five minutes. Beat the
egg yolk and slowly beat it into the hot
soup, stirring constantly. Serve immediately. Serves 3.

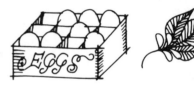

LEMON-RICE RING

½ cup rice	4 eggs, separated
½ teaspoon salt	2 tablespoons Sucaryl Solution
½ cup boiling water	1 tablespoon lemon rind
2½ cups skim milk	2 tablespoons lemon juice
1 tablespoon unflavored gelatin	1 teaspoon vanilla
¼ cup cold water	

Combine rice, salt and boiling water in
the top of a double boiler; bring to a boil
and cook about 2 minutes. Add milk,
cook 10 minutes more. Soften gelatin in
cold water, and set aside. Combine egg
yolks, Sucaryl, lemon rind and juice,
and vanilla. Add some of the hot rice
mixture to the egg yolk mixture, then
pour the egg yolk mixture back into the
rice and cook 5 minutes more, stirring.
Remove from heat, stir in softened
gelatin until dissolved. Chill slightly.
Beat egg whites until stiff, fold into rice
mixture. Spoon into a 2-quart ring mold
and chill until set. Serves 8.

PHOTOGRAPH: ABBOTT LABORATORIES

THURSDAY
THIRD WEEK

BREAKFAST
½ cup Pineapple-grapefruit Juice
1 Soft Boiled Egg
1 slice Raisin Toast with
1 teaspoon Dietetic Grape Jelly
Coffee or Tea

LUNCHEON
1 cup canned Chicken Noodle Soup
Open-face Grilled Cheese and Bacon
Sandwich: 1 slice Bread, 1 slice
American Cheese, 1 slice crisp cooked Bacon
6 Asparagus Spears
Dessert: 2 Pear Halves, water-pack or rinsed
Coffee or Tea

DINNER
½ small Cantaloupe
*Meat Balls in Tomato Sauce
½ cup Sliced Carrots, cooked
½ cup Mashed Potatoes
Salad: Lettuce Wedge, thin-sliced Green
Pepper, dash of Wine Vinegar
*Dessert: Cranberry Whip
Coffee or Tea

MEAT BALLS IN TOMATO SAUCE

1 onion, sliced	½ teaspoon salt
2 tablespoons oil	¼ teaspoon pepper
1 pound ground beef	1 slice white bread
	1 can tomato sauce

Sauté sliced onion in the oil, using a small skillet. Meanwhile, salt and pepper the ground beef. Wet the slice of bread with water and crumble up into beef. Add ¼ cup additional water and mix through until chunks of bread disappear. Form into small balls and brown in remaining oil, turning constantly. Cover meat balls with tomato sauce, and simmer with tight lid for 20 minutes. Serves 4.

CRANBERRY WHIP

2 cups cranberries	¼ cup non-fat dry milk
1 cup water	
2 tablespoons Sucaryl Solution	¼ cup iced water
2 envelopes Orange D-Zerta Gelatin	

Cook cranberries, water and Sucaryl until skins pop. Drain, saving both liquid and berries; add enough water to make 1½ cups. Stir in gelatin until dissolved. Chill until mixture begins to set, then beat until frothy. Beat dry milk and iced water until consistency of whipped cream, and fold into gelatin mixture. Fold in cooked cranberries. Chill until mixture begins to set. Pile into parfait glasses. Serves 6.

PHOTOGRAPH: ABBOTT LABORATORIES

FRIDAY
THIRD WEEK

BREAKFAST
½ cup Orange Juice
1 slice Raisin Bread, topped with
¼ cup Cottage Cheese, sprinkled with
Grated Orange Rind, dash of cinnamon,
and broiled 2 minutes
Coffee or Tea

LUNCHEON
½ cup Cranberry Juice Cocktail
*Chicken Salad
Dessert: 2 Apricot Halves, water-pack,
1 teaspoon Raisins
Coffee or Tea

DINNER
1 cup Vegetable Soup
*Fillet of Sole/Ginger Ale
½ cup Spinach, dash of nutmeg
½ cup cooked Yellow Squash
Salad: Wedge of Lettuce, 1 teaspoon
Chopped Chives
Italian-type Dietetic Dressing
Dessert: Lemon-Sherry Soufflé
Coffee or Tea

CHICKEN SALAD

½ cup cubed cooked chicken	2 teaspoons mayonnaise-type salad dressing
¼ cup diced celery	Shredded lettuce
¼ cup seedless grapes	½ sliced tomato

Combine the chicken, celery, grapes, and salad dressing. Mound on a bed of shredded lettuce. Garnish with sliced tomato.

FILLET OF SOLE/GINGER ALE

1 cup low-calorie ginger ale	1 teaspoon parsley flakes
1 tablespoon butter	1 tablespoon sour cream
1 small grated onion	Salt
1 bay leaf	Pepper
6 finely sliced mushrooms	1 pound fillet of sole

In a saucepan, combine ginger ale, butter, onion, bay leaf, mushrooms, and parsley flakes. Simmer for five minutes, reducing volume. Beat sour cream into this sauce. Salt and pepper fillets, and arrange in a shallow baking pan. Pour sauce over and bake for 20 minutes in 350° oven. Serves 3.

LEMON-SHERRY SOUFFLÉ

2 tablespoons flour	2 tablespoons lemon juice
½ teaspoon cinnamon	1 cup skim milk
½ teaspoon salt	1½ tablespoons Sucaryl Solution
1 egg, plus 2 egg yolks	2 egg whites, stiffly beaten
2 tablespoons sherry	

In a small bowl, combine flour, cinnamon and salt. In another bowl, combine 1 egg and 2 egg yolks, sherry, lemon juice, milk and Sucaryl. Beat this mixture into the dry ingredients. Fold in stiffly beaten egg whites. Pour into a lightly buttered soufflé dish, set in a pan of water and bake in 350° oven for 30 minutes. Serve warm or chilled. Serves 6.

SATURDAY
THIRD WEEK

BREAKFAST
½ Sliced Orange
1 Scrambled Egg, with
1 slice Crumbled Bacon in it,
on ½ English Muffin
Coffee or Tea

LUNCHEON
1 cup Bouillon, pinch dried parsley
*Broiled Butterfly Shrimp
½ cup Cole Slaw
Dessert: ½ cup unsweetened Applesauce,
sprinkled with a dash of cinnamon
Coffee or Tea

DINNER
1 cup canned Onion Soup, topped with
1 teaspoon Parmesan Cheese
*Veal Scallopini, 4-ounce portion
½ cup Spaghetti, with ¼ cup Tomato Puree
6 Asparagus Spears
Salad: Shredded Lettuce, Sliced Cucumber,
1 tablespoon Chives, with a
dash of Wine Vinegar
*Dessert: Peach Crème Ambrosia
Coffee or Tea

BROILED BUTTERFLY SHRIMP

4 ounces large shrimp, peeled and cleaned with tails on	Garlic salt Paprika Lemon wedge
1 tablespoon melted butter	

Split the shrimp into butterfly shape. Brush with melted butter, season with garlic salt and paprika. Broil for 3 minutes on each side. Serve with lemon wedge.

VEAL SCALLOPINI

1 pound veal scallopini slices	1 teaspoon oregano
1/4 cup flour	1/2 teaspon salt
2 tablespoons butter	1/4 teaspoon pepper
2 cups tomato juice	1/4 teaspoon garlic powder

Lightly flour veal slices. Brown in skillet with melted butter. Pour tomato juice over veal and add oregano, salt, pepper, and garlic powder. Cover and cook for about 15 minutes on low flame. Serves 4.

PEACH CRÈME AMBROSIA

4 eggs, separated	1/2 cup white wine
2 tablespoons Sucaryl Solution	1 tablespoon unflavored gelatin
1 pound can sliced peaches, Sucaryl sweetened	1/2 cup cold water
	1/2 cup shredded coconut
2 tablespoons lemon juice	

Combine egg yolks and Sucaryl, beat until light and fluffy. Drain peaches and crush. Add peach pulp, lemon juice and wine to egg yolk mixture. Cook in top of a double boiler, over hot water, until thick. Soften gelatin in cold water; add to cooked mixture, stirring to dissolve. Cool, stirring occasionally. When thick, add stiffly beaten egg whites. Fold in coconut. Spoon into serving dish and garnish with sliced peaches. Serves 8.

PHOTOGRAPH: ABBOTT LABORATORIES

SUNDAY THIRD WEEK

BREAKFAST
½ Grapefruit
1 cup Corn Flakes, several fresh
whole Strawberries
½ cup Skim Milk
Coffee or Tea

LUNCHEON
*Chicken Egg Drop Soup
*Sweet & Sour Tuna on
1 ounce Chow Mein Noodles, canned
Dessert: Orange D-Zerta Gelatin
Coffee or Tea

DINNER
¼ Cantaloupe
*Spring Lamb Curry, on
½ cup Rice
½ cup Whole Green Beans
Salad: Lettuce cup, three thick
slices of Tomato
*Dessert: Banana Parfait Pudding
Coffee or Tea

SPRING LAMB CURRY

1½ pounds bone-less lamb, cubed	1 10½-ounce can mushroom gravy
1 onion, chopped	¼ cup water
2 celery stalks, chopped	1 tablespoon tomato paste
1 clove garlic, minced	2 teaspoons curry powder
2 tablespoons butter	Dash salt
	Dash pepper

Trim lamb to remove excess fat. In large skillet, brown lamb and cook onion, celery, and garlic in butter. Stir in gravy, water, tomato paste, curry powder, salt, and pepper. Cover. Simmer over low heat about 1 hour, or until meat is tender. Serves 6.

CHICKEN EGG DROP SOUP

1 quart clear chicken soup	1 egg, beaten lightly with fork

Into the quart of rapidly boiling chicken soup, stir the beaten egg. Continue stirring as strings of egg whirl about. Serve immediately.

SWEET & SOUR TUNA

1 13½-ounce can water-pack pineapple chunks	1 teaspoon Sucaryl
1 cup green pepper squares	2 tablespoons vinegar
1 cup diagonally sliced celery	1 tablespoon soy sauce
2 tablespoons butter	1 can onion soup, undiluted
2 tablespoons cornstarch	2 cans tuna, water-pack

Drain pineapple, reserving liquid. Sauté pineapple, green pepper and celery in butter until vegetables are tender (about 5 minutes). Blend cornstarch, Sucaryl, vinegar, soy sauce and ⅔ cup pineapple juice. Poor into pineapple-vegetable mixture along with soup. Cook, stirring constantly, until thickened and clear. Add drained tuna chunks and heat through, spooning sauce gently over tuna to keep in large pieces. Serve immediately over chow mein noodles that have been heated for 3 minutes in a moderate oven. Serves 6.

BANANA PARFAIT PUDDING

1 envelope (4 serving size) low-calorie vanilla pudding (D-Zerta) prepared with non-fat milk	1 banana

Spoon prepared vanilla pudding into parfait glasses, alternating with thin slices of banana. Top with one banana slice. Serves 4.

PHOTOGRAPH: S & W

MONDAY
FOURTH WEEK

BREAKFAST
½ cup Orange Juice
*Jelly Omelet
Coffee or Tea

LUNCHEON
½ cup Apple Juice
Open-Faced Cheeseburger: 3 ounces lean
Ground Beef, 1 ounce Cheese
½ Broiled Tomato, pinch of oregano
*Dessert: ½ cup Mandarin Ambrosia
Coffee or Tea

DINNER
1 cup Clam Chowder, Manhattan style
*Fish Stick and Green Bean Casserole
Salad: Celery Sticks, Cucumber Sticks,
Radish Roses and 1 tablespoon
Cottage Cheese
*Dessert: 1 slice Chocolate Chip Angel
Food Cake, 2" Segment
Coffee or Tea

JELLY OMELET

1 egg, beaten	1 tablespoon dietetic raspberry jelly

Pour beaten egg into lightly buttered skillet, and cook until set. Flip onto plate, cover ½ with jelly and fold over. Serve immediately.

MANDARIN AMBROSIA

1 can mandarin oranges, small size	1 tablespoon grated coconut
1 tablespoon grated lemon rind	

In dessert dishes, spoon orange segments and juice. Sprinkle with grated lemon rind and top with grated coconut. Serves 2.

FISH STICK AND GREEN BEAN CASSEROLE

1 10-ounce package frozen french style green beans, thawed	¾ teaspoon salt ¼ teaspoon garlic powder ⅛ teaspoon crushed rosemary
1 1-pound can stewed tomatoes	1 8-ounce package frozen precooked fish sticks
2 tablespoons all-purpose flour	

Place green beans in a greased shallow casserole. Blend tomatoes with flour and seasonings; pour over green beans. Cover and bake in 375° oven for 30 minutes. Remove cover. Arrange fish sticks over top; return to oven and bake 10 minutes longer. Serves 3.

CHOCOLATE CHIP ANGEL FOOD CAKE

1 box angel food cake mix	1 cup chocolate chips

Mix angel food cake as directed, and fold in chocolate chips before baking.

PHOTOGRAPH: GENERAL FOODS

TUESDAY
FOURTH WEEK

BREAKFAST
½ cup Orange and Grapefruit Segments,
water-pack
1 Poached Egg, on
1 Slice Rye Toast
Coffee or Tea

LUNCHEON
*1 cup Tomato/Bouillon Soup, dash of basil
*Crabmeat Salad
6 Asparagus Spears
Dessert: ½ cup Applesauce, unsweetened,
1 teaspoon Raisins
Coffee or Tea

DINNER
1 cup condensed Cream of Celery Soup,
made with water
*Breast of Chicken with Pineapple
½ cup Rice
2 Broccoli Stalks
Salad: Chicory, Cucumber Slices, Bib
Lettuce, Wine Vinegar Dressing
*Dessert: Chocolate Mousse
Coffee or Tea

TOMATO/BOUILLON SOUP

½ cup tomato juice   1 teaspoon lemon
½ cup bouillon   juice
                     Pinch of basil

Heat ingredients together and serve with
lemon slices.

CRABMEAT SALAD

½ can (4 ounces)   ½ teaspoon grated
crabmeat, flaked   lemon rind
2 stalks celery,   1 tablespoon
diced fine   mayonnaise-type
¼ green pepper,   salad dressing
diced fine

Toss ingredients together and serve on
crisp lettuce cup.

BREAST OF CHICKEN WITH PINEAPPLE

6 boneless chicken   ¼ teaspoon ground
breasts   ginger
Salt   1 13½-ounce can
3 tablespoons flour   pineapple chunks
2 tablespoons
cooking oil

Flatten chicken breasts with a cleaver.
Sprinkle with salt and flour. Brown very
lightly on both sides in hot oil in a
skillet. Cover and cook for 20 minutes,
or until tender. Remove chicken from
skillet. Add 1 tablespoon flour and the
ginger to drippings in skillet. To syrup
drained from pineapple, add enough
water to make ¾ cup; stir into flour
mixture in skillet. Cook over low heat,
stirring until smooth. Add pineapple
chunks and warm through. Add chicken
and simmer until chicken is done.
Serves 6.

CHOCOLATE MOUSSE

2 ounces bitter   1 teaspoon rum
chocolate   flavoring
3 tablespoons   2 eggs, separated
boiling water
1 tablespoon
Sucaryl Solution

Grate chocolate and place in a blender.
Add boiling water, Sucaryl and rum
flavoring; blend for 1 minute. Add egg
yolks. Beat egg whites until stiff. Fold
chocolate mixture into egg whites.
Spoon into dessert dishes and chill until
firm. Serves 4.

PHOTOGRAPH: PINEAPPLE GROWERS ASSOCIATION

WEDNESDAY
FOURTH WEEK

BREAKFAST
½ cup Plums, dietetic pack
1 slice French Toast, with
1 teaspoon Dietetic Blueberry Jelly
Coffee or Tea

LUNCHEON
1 cup Vegetable Soup
*Curried Rice/Ham Tomatoes
½ cup Cole Slaw
Dessert: ½ Peach molded in
Lime D-Zerta Gelatin
Coffee or Tea

DINNER
1 cup Onion Soup, with
1 teaspoon Parmesan Cheese
*Florentine Steak
½ cup Spinach
½ cup Summer Squash
Salad: Wedge of Lettuce with Pimento
Strip, Wine Vinegar Dressing
*Dessert: Orange-Pineapple Sherbet
Coffee or Tea

FLORENTINE STEAK

Flank steak	Salt
1 tablespoon olive oil	Freshly ground pepper

Rub flank steak with olive oil, salt and pepper. Let stand at room temperature an hour. Broil quickly on both sides and slice on the diagonal. Serve with lemon wedges. Four-ounce serving each.

CURRIED RICE/HAM TOMATOES

1 6-ounce box Uncle Ben's Curried Rice, cooked	1 cup sour cream
	4 teaspoons soy sauce
6 large firm tomatoes	3 tablespoons chopped parsley
1 tablespoon butter	2 tablespoons grated sharp cheese
1 onion, chopped fine	2 tablespoons bread crumbs
1 tablespoon flour	
8 ounces cooked ham, shredded fine	

Remove a thin slice from stem end of each tomato and scoop out pulp. Place in a lightly greased baking pan. Sauté onions in butter, add flour and blend. Combine rice with onions, ham, sour cream, soy sauce and parsley. Fill tomatoes with mixture. Mix grated cheese and bread crumbs and sprinkle over stuffed tomatoes. Bake in preheated oven at 400° for 40 minutes. Serves 6.

 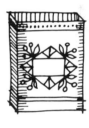 

ORANGE-PINEAPPLE SHERBET

1 6-ounce can frozen unsweetened orange juice concentrate	3½ cups cold water
	2 tablespoons Sucaryl Solution
1 6-ounce can frozen unsweetened pineapple juice concentrate	1 cup non-fat dry milk solids

Put all ingredients into a large mixing bowl and beat just enough to blend thoroughly. Pour into ice cube trays; freeze 1 to 2 hours until half frozen. Remove to large chilled mixer bowl; beat on low speed until mixture is softened, then beat on high speed 3 to 5 minutes until creamy but not liquid. Pour into freezer containers or ice cube trays. Freeze until ready to serve. Makes 20 ½-cup servings.

PHOTOGRAPH: UNCLE BEN'S INC.

THURSDAY
FOURTH WEEK

BREAKFAST
½ Sliced Orange
*Ranch Egg, served on
1 slice Canadian Bacon
Coffee or Tea

LUNCHEON
1 cup Cold Borscht, with floating
diced cucumber
*Chicken Livers & Mushrooms, on
1 slice White Toast
½ cup Coleslaw
*Dessert: Orange-Apricot Coupe
Coffee or Tea

DINNER
1 cup Clam Chowder, Manhattan Style
*Stuffed Lobster Tails
½ cup Tiny Whole Carrots, grated
orange rind
1 small Baked Potato, with
1 teaspoon Butter
Salad: 3 thick Tomato Slices, sprinkled with
Chives, and dash of Wine Vinegar
Dessert: 1 thin slice Sponge Cake
Coffee or Tea

RANCH EGG

1 egg, beaten	1 tablespoon grated
2 tablespoons	onion
chopped green	1 tablespoon diced
pepper	pimento

Mix green pepper, onion, and pimiento into beaten egg. Pour into a lightly buttered skillet and scramble. Serve at once on a slice of cooked Canadian bacon.

CHICKEN LIVERS AND MUSHROOMS

¼ pound chicken livers, quartered	1 can (4 oz.) sliced mushrooms
1 thinly sliced onion	1 teaspoon cornstarch
1 tablespoon butter	1 teaspoon lemon juice

Sauté cut-up livers and onions in butter. Add drained mushrooms, reserving liquid. Blend cornstarch and lemon juice into mushroom liquid until smooth, and then pour over livers. Cook and stir over low heat for several minutes until livers are cooked through. Serve on toast points to 2.

ORANGE-APRICOT COUPE

1 can apricot halves, dietetic pack	1 package Orange D-Zerta Gelatin

Spoon apricot halves into four dessert coupes. Mix D-Zerta Gelatin according to directions, using the apricot liquid as part of the water used. Pour over apricots. Chill for several hours. Serves 4.

STUFFED LOBSTER TAILS

6 boiled lobster tails	⅓ cup finely chopped onions
4 cups Corn Flakes or 1 cup packaged Corn Flake Crumbs	⅓ cup butter
	1 tablespoon lemon juice

Cut under-shell from lobster tails; split meat down the center. Loosen meat from shells (do not remove). If using Corn Flakes, crush into fine crumbs. Sauté onion in butter until tender. Combine with Corn Flake Crumbs and lemon juice. Mix well. Fill each lobster cavity with stuffing. Place on broiler rack. Sprinkle with melted butter. Broil, with top of lobster 4 inches from heat, until meat and stuffing are lightly browned and heated through. Garnish with lemon wedges and serve to 6.

PHOTOGRAPH: KELLOGG COMPANY

FRIDAY
FOURTH WEEK

BREAKFAST

½ cup Pineapple-Grapefruit Juice
1 slice Raisin Toast, topped with
2 tablespoons Cottage Cheese,
    grated Orange Rind, broiled
Coffee or Tea

LUNCHEON

¼ Cantaloupe
*Salmon Suey, on
1 ounce Chinese Noodles, canned
Dessert: Lemon D-Zerta Gelatin
Coffee or Tea

DINNER

Shrimp Cocktail, 4 large shrimp
*Shoulder of Veal Roast, 2 thin slices
½ cup Mashed Potatoes
½ cup Pickled Beets
Salad: Wedge of Lettuce, Sliced Tomato,
    Dietetic French Dressing
*Dessert: Peaches Cardinale
Coffee or Tea

SALMON SUEY

2 tablespoons oil	1 teaspoon soy sauce
½ cup chopped onion	
½ cup chopped celery	½ green pepper, cut into thin strips
1 1-pound can salmon	1 tablespoon cornstarch
½ teaspoon salt	¼ cup water
¼ teaspoon pepper	1 1-pound can bean sprouts, drained
1 teaspoon sugar	

In a skillet heat oil and sauté onion and celery for 5 minutes, or until onion is golden. Add salmon liquid from can, the salt, pepper, sugar, soy sauce, and green pepper. Cover and simmer for 10 minutes. Blend cornstarch with the water and stir into mixture in skillet. Cook over low heat, stirring until sauce is slightly thickened. Stir in bean sprouts. Drain, flake and add the salmon. Cover and simmer 5 minutes more. Serve on Chinese noodles. Serves 4.

SHOULDER OF VEAL ROAST

2 pounds shoulder of veal roast, boned, rolled, and tied	1 cup beef bouillon
	3 teaspoons paprika
2 onions, sliced thin	1 can sauerkraut, drained
1 clove garlic, minced	1 teaspoon caraway seeds
½ teaspoon salt	

In a large covered pot, combine the onions, garlic, salt, caraway seeds and bouillon. Simmer for 5 minutes. Add the veal. Add sauerkraut and paprika. Cover and simmer for 2 hours, or until tender. Serves 6.

PEACHES CARDINALE

½ cup raspberries	2 tablespoons brandy
½ cup strawberries	
1 tablespoon Sucaryl Solution	1 1-pound can Sucaryl-sweetened peach halves
½ teaspoon cornstarch	

Mash raspberries and strawberries and combine in small sauce pan. Stir in Sucaryl blended with cornstarch. Bring to a boil, cook and stir until thickened. Stir in brandy. Add drained peach halves, basting peaches with the sauce. Serve hot to 6.

PHOTOGRAPH: CANNED SALMON INSTITUTE

SATURDAY FOURTH WEEK

BREAKFAST
½ cup Orange Juice
*Scrambled Egg with Cottage Cheese
Coffee or Tea

LUNCHEON
1 cup Bouillon, several Croutons
1 Broiled Lamb Chop, well-trimmed
shoulder cut
½ cup Wax Beans
½ cup Cauliflower
Dessert: ½ cup unsweetened Applesauce
Coffee or Tea

DINNER
½ cup Fruit Salad, dietetic pack
*Spicy Meat Loaf
½ cup Spinach
1 ear Corn, with
1 teaspoon butter
Salad: ½ cup Coleslaw
*Dessert: Orange Cranberry Tart
Coffee or Tea

SCRAMBLED EGG WITH COTTAGE CHEESE

1 egg	2 tablespoons
1 tablespoon water	cottage cheese

Beat egg and water together lightly. Pour into a buttered skillet and stir in cottage cheese as egg is setting. Serve immediately.

SPICY MEAT LOAF

1¼ pounds lean ground round beef	1 teaspoon salt
	½ teaspoon pepper
1 egg, beaten	3 tablespoons grated onion
3 tablespoons cold water	1 tablespoon ketchup mixed with 1 tablespoon mustard
3 tablespoons ketchup	

Mix ground beef, egg, cold water, ketchup, salt, pepper, and grated onion together. Fill small loaf pan and bake in 350° oven for 45 minutes. Spread ketchup-mustard mixture over top and bake another 45 minutes, or until done to your taste. Serves 5.

ORANGE-CRANBERRY TARTS

Pastry mix for a 9-inch pie shell	1 tablespoon cornstarch
2 cups cranberries	1 tablespoon unflavored gelatin
½ cup orange juice	
½ cup water	¼ cup cold water
3 tablespoons Sucaryl Solution	1 cup orange sections

Mix and roll pastry. Cut to fit 10 small tart pans. Bake in 425° oven for 10 minutes. Cool. Combine cranberries, orange juice and water in a small saucepan and cook until the skins pop. Force through a sieve. Add Sucaryl and combine a little of the fruit mixture with cornstarch to make a smooth paste. Return the paste to the fruit mixture and cook, stirring constantly until thick and smooth. Soften gelatin in cold water and add to the hot fruit mixture, stirring to dissolve gelatin. Chill until almost set. Spoon into tart shells and top with sections of orange. Makes 10 tarts.

PHOTOGRAPH: ABBOTT LABORATORIES

SUNDAY FOURTH WEEK

BREAKFAST
½ Grapefruit
1 cup Puffed Rice, with
½ cup Skim Milk
½ sliced Banana
Coffee or Tea

LUNCHEON
½ cup Tomato Juice, dash of
Worcestershire sauce
*Apple Soufflé
½ cup Peas
1 slice Raisin Toast, spread with
1 teaspoon Butter
Dessert: ½ cup Sliced Peaches, water-pack
Coffee or Tea

DINNER
1 cup Vegetable Soup
Turkey, roasted, 4-ounce serving
½ cup Wild Rice
½ cup String Beans
Spiced Apple Slice
*Dessert: Orange Chiffon Pie
Coffee or Tea

APPLE SOUFFLÉ

4 eggs	1 cup unsweetened
1 teaspoon soft	applesauce
shortening	3 tablespoons
½ teaspoon	flour
Adolph's Granu-	2 teaspoons
lated Sugar	Adolph's Granu-
Substitute	lated Sugar
½ teaspoon	Substitute
cinnamon	

Separate eggs. Lightly grease a 1-quart soufflé dish with shortening. Mix ½ teaspoon sugar substitute with ½ teaspoon cinnamon and coat sides and bottom of dish with this mixture. In a small saucepan, combine applesauce and flour, cook over low heat, stirring constantly until mixture thickens. Remove from heat and blend in the rest of the sugar substitute. Beat egg yolks and stir into mixture. Cool. Meanwhile, beat egg whites stiff enough to hold their shape and lightly fold into fruit mixture until almost completely blended. Pour into soufflé dish and bake in 350° oven for 35 minutes, until top is firm and golden. Serves 6.

ORANGE CHIFFON PIE

⅓ cup unsweetened	1 envelope (1
orange juice	tablespoon) un-
4 teaspoons	flavored gelatin
Sucaryl Solution	1 9-inch baked,
¼ cup cold water	cooled pastry
Dash of salt	shell
3 eggs, separated	

In top of double boiler, combine juice, Sucaryl, salt and egg yolks. Cook over hot water until mixture coats the spoon. Remove from heat. Soften gelatin in cold water and add to juice mixture, stirring to dissolve. Chill until mixture begins to thicken. Beat egg whites until stiff peaks form, fold into thickened fruit juice mixture. Spoon into pastry shell. Chill until set. Garnish with low-calorie whipped topping. Serves 6.

PHOTOGRAPH: LORD MOTT

FOOD BRAND INDEX

Do you sometimes wonder how many calories are in the prepared foods that you buy? Here is a special index of food brand calorie counts of outstanding food products with national distribution. It has been compiled with the cooperation of the companies listed, in an effort to provide you with information that is not required to appear on package labels.

Here is an opportunity to evaluate any substitutions you may desire to make in your diet, so that you may know what you are eating. The General Calorie Count Index following this section will be helpful wherever general information is desired.

To use the Food Brand Index most effectively, look for the product under its brand name or under the manufacturer's name easily found on the food label. Pay particular attention to the portion listed for each calorie count. This informative service for the reader has been prepared in the hope that knowledge, rather than haphazard appetites, will be used in the selection of food for the dieters in your family.

PHOTOGRAPH: ABBOTT LABORATORIES

FOOD BRAND CALORIE COUNT

On this and the following pages, foods are listed by their brand names, under the name of the manufacturer. Calorie counts are for the amount specified in each instance. You will note that in some cases a particular method of preparation has been specified, also.

Food	Cal.	Quantity

ARNOLD BAKERS, INC.

Food	Cal.	Quantity
1 # Brick Oven White Bread	66	per slice
1 # Brick Oven Wheat Bread	64	"
Hearthstone White Bread	87	"
Hearthstone Wheat Bread	85	"
Raisin Tea Bread	69	"
2 # Brick Oven White Bread	94	"
Dutch Egg Bread	90	"
Butter Rolls	63	per roll
Barbeque Rolls	113	"
Butter Parkers	59	"
Hot Dog Rolls	100	"
Dutch Egg Buns	109	"

BEECH-NUT BABY FOODS

Strained Juices

Food	Cal.	Quantity
Apple	60	per container
Apple-Cherry	60	"
Apple-Grape	70	"

Food	Cal.	Quantity
Mixed Fruit (from concentrates)	60	per container
Orange (from concentrates)	70	"
Orange-Apple (from concentrates)	80	"
Orange-Apricot (from concentrates)	80	"
Orange-Banana (from concentrates)	90	"
Orange-Pineapple (from concentrates)	70	"
Prune-Orange (from concentrates)	80	"

Strained Fruits

Food	Cal.	Quantity
Apples & Apricots	121	per container
Applesauce	100	"
Applesauce & Cherries	120	"
Applesauce & Raspberries	130	"

Apricots with
  Tapioca ..... 90...per container
Bananas with
  Tapioca .....100...   "
Bananas &
  Pineapple
  with Tapioca ..110...   "
Peaches ....117...   "
Pears .... 80...   "
Pears &
  Pineapple ....100...   "
Plums with
  Tapioca .....110...   "
Prunes with
  Tapioca .....110...   "

Strained Vegetables

Carrots .... 40...per container
Carrots in
  Butter Sauce.. 69...   "
Creamed Corn .. 90...   "
Garden
  Vegetables ... 60...   "
Green Beans .... 36...   "
Green Beans in
  Butter Sauce.. 60...   "
Peas .... 70...   "
Peas in Butter
  Sauce .... 80...   "
Squash .... 44...   "
Squash in Butter
  Sauce .... 60...   "
Sweet Potatoes .. 70...   "
Sweet Potatoes in
  Butter Sauce.. 70...   "

Strained Meats & Egg Yolks

Beef .... 101...per container
Chicken ......100...   "
Ham ....100...   "
Lamb .... 92...   "
Pork ....100...   "
Turkey ....103...   "
Veal ....100...   "
Egg Yolks ......190...   "

Strained High Meat Dinners

Beef ....120...per container

Chicken ....110...per container
Ham ....130...   "
Turkey ....100...   "
Veal .... 90...   "

Strained Dinners & Soups

Beef & Noodles.. 60...per container
Cereal, Egg Yolks
  & Bacon .....110...   "
Chicken Noodle.. 50...   "
Chicken with
  Vegetables ... 60...   "
Macaroni, Tomato
  Sauce, Beef
  & Bacon ..... 90...   "
Turkey & Rice ... 70...   "
Vegetables &
  Bacon .... 70...   "
Vegetables &
  Beef .... 70...   "
Vegetables &
  Ham .... 70...   "
Vegetables &
  Lamb .... 70...   "
Vegetables &
  Liver .... 50...   "
Vegetable Soup.. 50...   "
Mixed Cereal with
  Fruit .... 90...   "
Oatmeal with
  Fruit .... 90...   "

Strained Desserts

Apple Betty .....110...per container
Caramel
  Pudding .....120...   "
Chocolate
  Custard .....130...   "
Creamed Cottage
  Cheese with
  Pineapple
  Juice ....110...   "
Custard
  Pudding .....100...   "
Fruit Dessert with
  Tapioca .....110...   "
Orange Pineapple
  Dessert ......130...   "

Peach Melba . . . 120 . . . per container
Pineapple
   Dessert . . . . . . 130 . . .   "

Junior Fruits
Apples &
   Apricots . . . . . 190 . . . per container
Applesauce . . . . . 160 . . .   "
Applesauce &
   Cherries . . . . . 190 . . .   "
Applesauce &
   Raspberries . . 200 . . .   "
Apricots with
   Tapioca . . . . . 160 . . .   "
Bananas &
   Pineapple with
   Tapioca . . . . 180 . . .   "
Peaches . . . . 190 . . .   "
Pears . . . . 140 . . .   "
Pears &
   Pineapple . . . . 170 . . .   "
Plums with
   Tapioca . . . . 180 . . .   "
Prunes with
   Tapioca . . . . 190 . . .   "

Junior Vegetables
Carrots . . . . 70 . . . per container
Carrots in Butter
   Sauce . . . . 120 . . .   "
Creamed Corn . . 150 . . .   "
Green Beans . . . . 70 . . .   "
Green Beans in
   Butter Sauce . . 80 . . .   "
Peas in Butter
   Sauce . . . . . . 120 . . .   "
Squash . . . . 70 . . .   "
Squash in Butter
   Sauce . . . . 90 . . .   "
Sweet Potatoes . . 120 . . .   "
Sweet Potatoes in
   Butter Sauce . . 130 . . .   "

Junior High Meat Dinners
Beef . . . . 119 . . . per container
Chicken . . . . 100 . . .   "
Ham . . . . 120 . . .   "
Turkey . . . . 100 . . .   "
Veal . . . . 100 . . .   "

Junior Meats
Beef . . . . 110 . . . per container
Chicken . . . . 100 . . .   "
Chicken Sticks . . 140 . . .   "
Meat Sticks . . . . 150 . . .   "
Lamb . . . . 100 . . .   "
Pork . . . . 110 . . .   "
Turkey . . . . 100 . . .   "
Veal . . . . 110 . . .   "

Junior Dinners & Soups
Beef & Noodles . . 110 . . . per container
Cereal, Egg Yolks
   & Bacon . . . . . 170 . . .   "
Chicken Noodle . . 80 . . .   "
Chicken with
   Vegetables . . . 80 . . .   "
Lamb &
   Noodles . . . . . 130 . . .   "
Macaroni &
   Bacon . . . . 150 . . .   "
Macaroni &
   Beef with
   Vegetables . . . 110 . . .   "
Spaghetti, Tomato
   Sauce &
   Beef . . . . 140 . . .   "
Split Peas,
   Vegetables
   & Ham . . . . . . 130 . . .   "
Turkey &
   Rice with
   Vegetables . . . 80 . . .   "
Vegetables &
   Bacon . . . . 120 . . .   "
Vegetables &
   Beef . . . . 120 . .   "
Vegetables &
   Lamb . . . . 120 . . .   "
Vegetables &
   Liver . . . . 90 . . .   "
Vegetable Soup . . 80 . . .   "

Junior Desserts
Apple Betty . . . . . 200 . . . per container
Banana Dessert . . 180 . . .   "
Caramel
   Pudding . . . . . 200 . . .   "

Creamed Cottage
  Cheese with
  Pineapple ....170...per container
Custard
  Pudding .....200...   ″
Fruit Dessert with
  Tapioca .....190...   ″
Peach Melba ....180...   ″
Tropical Fruit
  Dessert ......180...   ″

BEST FOODS COMPANY
(Argo, Bosco, Fanning's H-O, Hell-
mann's, Karo, Mazola, Presto, Skippy)

Argo Corn
  Starch ...... 35...1 tbsp.
Best Foods
  Mustard with
  Horseradish .. 10...   ″
Bosco Milk
  Amplifier .... 55...   ″
Diet Mazola
  Imitation
  Margarine .... 50...   ″
Golden Griddle
  Pancake
  Syrup .... 50...   ″

Fanning's Bread
  and Butter
  Pickles ...... 45...100 grams

H-O Cream
  Enriched Farina
  (uncooked) ... 40...1 tbsp.
H-O Instant
  Oatmeal
  (uncooked) ...255...1 cup
H-O Old-Fashioned
  Oats
  (uncooked) ...255...   ″
H-O Quick Oats
  (uncooked) ...255...   ″

Hellmann's Family
  French
  Dressing ..... 65...1 tbsp.

Hellmann's Old
  Homestead
  Garlic French
  Dressing ..... 65... 1 tbsp.
Hellmann's Real
  Mayonnaise ..100...   ″
Hellmann's Sand-
  wich Spred ... 60...   ″
Hellmann's Spin
  Blend Salad
  Dressing ..... 55...   ″
Hellmann's Tartar
  Sauce .... 70...   ″

Karo All Purpose
  Syrup
  (Blue Label) .. 60...   ″
Karo Crystal-Clear
  Syrup
  (Red Label) ... 60...   ″
Karo Imitation
  Maple Syrup .. 55...   ″
Karo Pancake and
  Waffle Syrup .. 60...   ″

Mazola Corn Oil..125...1 tbsp.
Mazola
  Margarine ....100...   ″
Mazola
  Margarine,
  unsalted .....100...   ″

Nucoa
  Margarine ....100...   ″
Nucoa Soft
  Margarine .... 90...   ″

Old Manse
  Syrup .... 50...   ″

Presto Self-Rising
  Cake Flour ...400...1 cup

Skippy Creamy
  Peanut
  Butter .... 95...1 tbsp.
Skippy Super
  Chunk Peanut
  Butter .... 95...   ″

Skippy Dry
Roasted
Peanuts . . . . . 165 . . . 1 oz.
Skippy Dry
Roasted
Mixed Nuts . . . 170 . . . 1 oz.

THE BORDEN COMPANY

Borden's Danish
Margarine . . . . 100 . . . 1 tbsp.
Borden's Sour
Half and Half . . 20 . . .   "
Borden's Grated
Parmesan
Cheese . . . . . . 31 . . .   "
Borden's Grated
Romano
Cheese . . . . . . 31 . . .   "
Borden's Hemo,
Chocolate
Flavor . . . . 40 . . .   "

Tropical Brand
Crystallized
Ginger . . . . . . 97 . . . 1 oz.
Tropical Brand
Preserved
Ginger . . . . . . 88 . . .   "
Borden's Instant
Dutch
Chocolate
Flavored Mix . . 87 . . . 2 tsps.
                    undiluted
Borden's Sour
Cream . . . . . 29 . . . 1 tbsp.
Borden's Instant
Malted Milk,
Double
Malted . . . . . . 80 . . . 2 tsps.
                    undiluted
Borden's Homog-
enized Fluid
Milk . . . . 151 . . . 1 cup
Borden's Unsalted
Cottage
Cheese . . . . . . 195 . . .   "

Borden's Creamed
Cottage
Cheese . . . . . . 241 . . . 1 cup
Borden's
Chocolate
Flavored
Milk . . . . 209 . . .   "
Borden's Partially
Skimmed
Milk . . . . 122 . . .   "
Borden's
Chocolate
Flavored
Drink . . . . 181 . . .   "

None Such Ready-
to-Use Mince
Meat . . . . 225 . . . 3½ oz.
None Such
Condensed
Mince Meat . . 391 . . . 3½ oz.

Borden's Dutch
Flavored Choc-
olate Drink . . . 185 . . . 1 cup
Borden's Instant
Chocolate
Flavor Malted
Milk, Double
Malted . . . . . . 77 . . . 2 tsps.
                    undiluted
Eagle Brand
Sweetened
Condensed
Milk . . . . 1000 . . . 1 cup
Household
Brands
Sweetened
Condensed
Milk . . . . 1009 . . .   "

Borden's
Liederkranz
Brand
Cheese . . . . . 86 . . . 1 oz.
Borden's Eagle
Brand
Neufchatel
Cheese . . . . . . 73 . . .   "

Borden's Cream
  Cheese ...... 96 ... 1 oz.
Borden's Camem-
  bert Cheese .. 86 ... "
Borden's Swiss
  Style Yogurt .. 167 ... 1 cup

Borden's
  Cremora ..... 11 ... 1 tsp.
Borden's Eggnog
  (4.69% Milk-
  fat) .... 263 ... 1 cup
Borden's Eggnog
  (6% Milkfat) .. 302 ... "
Borden's Eggnog
  (8% Milkfat) .. 342 ... "

CAMPBELL'S SOUP COMPANY
**(Campbells, Franco-American,
Swanson, Pepperidge Farm)**

CAMPBELL'S
**Canned Condensed Soups, prepared
with water unless otherwise specified**
Asparagus,
  Cream of ..... 100 ... 10 ozs.
Bean with
  Bacon .... 200 ... "
Beef .... 100 ... "
Beef Broth
  (Bouillon) .... 35 ... "
Beef Noodle .... 90 ... "
Black Bean ..... 130 ... "
Celery, Cream
  of .... 110 ... "
Cheddar
  Cheese ...... 180 ... "
Chicken
  Broth .... 50 ... "
Chicken, Cream
  of .... 140 ... "
Chicken 'n
  Dumplings ... 120 ... "
Chicken Gumbo .. 70 ... "
Chicken
  Noodle ...... 90 ... "
Chicken
  Noodle-O's ... 90 ... "

Chicken with
  Rice .... 80 ... 10 ozs.
Chicken &
  Stars ...... 80 ... "
Chicken
  Vegetable .... 90 ... "
Chili Beef ..... 190 ... "
Clam Chowder
  (Manhattan
  Style) .... 100 ... "
Clam Chowder,
  New England .. 100 ... 10 ozs.
Clam Chowder,
  New England
  (made with
  milk) ...... 190 ... "
Consomme (Beef)
  Gelatin
  Added ...... 40 ... "
Curly Noodle with
  Chicken ..... 100 ... "
Golden Vegetable
  Noodle-O's ... 90 ... "
Green Pea ...... 180 ... "
Hot Dog Bean ... 210 ... "
Minestrone ..... 110 ... "
Mushroom, Cream
  of .... 150 ... "
Mushroom,
  Golden ...... 100 ... "
Noodles & Ground
  Beef .... 110 ... "
Onion .... 80 ... "
Oyster Stew .... 80 ... "
Oyster Stew (made
  with milk) .... 170 ... "
Pepper Pot ..... 130 ... "
Potato, Cream
  of .... 90 ... "
Potato, Cream of
  (made with
  water and
  milk) .... 140 ... "
Scotch Broth ... 100 ... "
Shrimp, Cream
  of .... 120 ... "
Shrimp, Cream of
  (made with milk) . 210 ... "

Split Pea with
  Ham . . . . .210. . .10 ozs.
Stockpot . . . . . . .120. . .   "
Tomato . . . . .110. . .   "
Tomato (made
  with milk) . . . .210. . .   "
Tomato-Beef
  Noodle-O's . . .160. . .   "
Tomato Bisque . .150. . .10 ozs.
Tomato Rice, Old
  Fashioned . . .140. . .   "
Turkey Noodle . . 90. . .   "
Turkey
  Vegetable . . . . 90. . .   "
Vegetable . . . . . .100. . .   "
Vegetable Beef . . 90. . .   "
Vegetable, Old
  Fashioned . . . 90. . .   "
Vegetarian
  Vegetable . . . . 90. . .   "

Canned Chunky Soups, undiluted
Chunky Beef . . . .210. . .9½ ozs.
Chunky
  Chicken . . . . .200. . .   "
Chunky Chicken
  with Rice . . . .160. . .   "
Chunky Clam
  Chowder
  (Manhattan
  Style) . . . . . . .160. . .   "
Chunky Sirloin
  Burger . . . . . .210. . .   "
Chunky Split Pea
  with Ham . . . .220. . .   "
Chunky Turkey . .160. . .9¼ ozs.
Chunky
  Vegetable . . . .140. . .9½ ozs.

**Canned Low Sodium Soups, undiluted,
individual service size**
Green Pea, Low
  Sodium . . . . .140. . .1 can
Mushroom, Cream
  of, Low
  Sodium . . . . .130. . .   "
Tomato, Low
  Sodium . . . . .100. . .   "

Turkey Noodle,
  Low Sodium . . 60. . .1 can
Vegetable, Low
  Sodium . . . . . 80. . .   "
Vegetable Beef,
  Low Sodium . . 80. . .   "

Canned Products
Barbecue Beans. .280. . .8 ozs.
Beans 'n Beef in
  Tomato
  Sauce . . . . . . .280. . .7½ ozs.
Beans & Franks
  in Tomato &
  Molasses
  Sauce . . . . . . .370. . .8 ozs.
Home Style
  Beans . . . . . . .300. . .   "
Old Fashioned
  Beans in
  Molasses and
  Brown Sugar
  Sauce . . . . . . .290. . .   "
Pork & Beans
  with Tomato
  Sauce . . . . . . .260. . .   "
Tomato Juice . . . 35. . .6 ozs.
"V-8" Cocktail
  Vegetable
  Juice . . . . 35. . .   "

**FRANCO-AMERICAN CANNED
PRODUCTS**
Beef Raviolios in
  Meat Sauce . .240. . .7½ ozs.
Elbow Macaroni &
  Cheese . . . . . .200. . .7¼ ozs.
Macaroni 'n Beef
  in Tomato
  Sauce . . . . . . .220. . .7½ ozs.
Macaroni &
  Cheese . . . . . .200. . .7¼ ozs.
Spaghetti in
  Tomato Sauce
  with Cheese . .180. . .7½ ozs.
Spaghetti 'n Beef
  in Tomato
  Sauce . . . . . . .250. . .   "

Spaghetti with
   Meatballs
   in Tomato
   Sauce . . . . . . .230. . .7¼ ozs.
"SpaghettiOs" in
   Tomato and
   Cheese
   Sauce . . . . . . .170. . .7½ ozs.
"SpaghettiOs"
   with Little
   Meatballs in
   Tomato
   Sauce . . . . . . .230. . .   "
"SpaghettiOs"
   with Sliced
   Franks in
   Tomato
   Sauce . . . . . . .260. . .   "
Beef Gravy . . . . . 35. . .2 ozs.
Brown Gravy with
   Onions . . . . . . 35. . .   "
Chicken Gravy . . 55. . .2 ozs.
Chicken Giblet
   Gravy . . . . 35. . .   "
Mushroom
   Gravy . . . . 35. . .   "

SWANSON CANNED PRODUCTS
Boned Chicken
   with Broth . . .110. . .2½ ozs.
Boned Turkey
   with Broth . . .110. . .   "
Chicken Spread. . 70. . .1 oz.
Beef Broth . . . . . 20. . .8 ozs.
Chicken Broth . . . 30. . .   "
Beef Stew . . . . . .190. . .7½ ozs.
Chicken Stew . . .180. . .   "
Chicken a la
   King . . . . .190. . .5¼ ozs.
Chicken &
   Dumplings . . .230. . .7½ ozs.
Chili Con Carne
   (with Beans) . .300. . .7¾ ozs.

SWANSON FROZEN PREPARED PRODUCTS
Swanson "TV" Brand Dinners
Beans and
   Franks . . . . . .550. . .1 dinner
Beef . . . . .370. . .   "
Chopped
   Sirloin . . . . . .460. . .   "
Filet of Ocean
   Fish . . . . .440. . .   "
Fish 'N' Chips . .450. . .   "
Fried Chicken . . .570. . .   "
Ham . . . . .380. . .   "
Macaroni and
   Beef . . . . . . .410. . .   "
Noodles and
   Chicken . . . . .380. . .   "
Salisbury Steak . .500. . .   "
Spaghetti and
   Meatballs . . . .320. . .   "
Swiss Steak . . . .380. . .   "
Turkey . . . . . . .360. . .   "
Veal
   Parmigiana . . .520. . .   "

International Dinners
Beef Enchilada . .570. . .1 dinner
Chinese . . . . . . .330. . .   "
Italian Style . . . .510. . .   "
Mexican Style . . .700. . .   "
Polynesian
   Style . . . . .510. . .   "

3 Course Dinners
Beef . . . . .540. . .1 dinner
Fried Chicken . . .670. . .   "
Meat Loaf . . . . . .540. . .   "
Mexican Style . . .620. . .   "
Salisbury Steak . .510. . .   "
Turkey . . . . .550. . .   "

Hungry-Man Dinners
Boneless
   Chicken . . . . .770. . .1 dinner
Fried Chicken . . .960. . .   "
Salisbury Steak . .930. . .   "
Turkey . . . . .690. . .   "

Meat Pies
Beef . . . . .430. . .1 pie
Chicken . . . . . .460. . . "
Turkey . . . . . . .450. . . "
Macaroni and
   Cheese . . . . . .230. . . "

Deep Dish Meat Pies
Beef . . . . .770. . .1 pie
Chicken . . . . . .750. . .1 pie
Turkey . . . . . . .760. . . "
Macaroni and
   Cheese . . . . . .480. . . "

"TV" Brand Entrees
Fried Chicken
   with Whipped
   Potatoes . . . . .380. . .1 entree
Meatballs with
   Brown Gravy
   and Whipped
   Potatoes . . . . .330. . . "
Meat Loaf with
   Tomato Sauce
   and Whipped
   Potatoes . . . . .320. . . "
Salisbury Steak
   with
   Crinkle-Cut
   Potatoes . . . . .370. . . "
Spaghetti in To-
   mato Sauce
   with Breaded
   Veal . . . . . . .290. . . "
Turkey • Gravy •
   Dressing with
   Whipped
   Potatoes . . . . .260. . . "

Frozen Breakfasts
French Toast with
   Link
   Sausages . . . .300. . .1 breakfast
Pancakes and Link
   Sausages . . . .480. . . "
Scrambled Eggs
   and Link
   Sausage with
   Coffee Cake . .420. . . "

International Entrees
Chinese Style
   (Chicken Chow
   Mein with
   Rice) . . . . . . .200. . .1 entree
English Style (Fish
   'n' Chips) . . . .300. . . "
Italian Style (Beef
   Ravioli with
   Meat Sauce
   and Apple
   Slices) . . . . . .280. . . "
Mexican Style
   (Beef Enchi-
   ladas with
   Refried
   Beans) . . . . . .450. . . "

Fried Chicken in Family Packs
Fried Chicken
   (6 or more
   pieces) . . . . . .300. . .1 package
Fried Chicken with
   Crinkle-Cut
   Potatoes . . . . .530. . . "

Frozen Chicken Parts
Livers . . . . .120. . .4 ozs.

PEPPERIDGE FARM PRODUCTS
Breads
French . . . . .150. . .2 ozs.
Italian . . . . .140. . . "
White, Large . . . . 75. . .1 slice
White,
   Sandwich . . . . 60. . . "
White, Sliced . . . 75. . . "
White, Toasting . . 85. . . "
White, Unsliced . .160. . .2 ozs.
White, Very Thin
   Sliced . . . . . . 45. . .1 slice

Rolls
Butterfly . . . . 60. . .each
Butter Crescent . .130. . . "
Club . . . . .120. . . "
Deli (Plain/
   Seeded) . . . . .160. . . "

Dinner . . . . 60 . . . each
Finger, White,
   (Poppy/
   Sesame) . . . . . 60 . . . "
French Rolls,
   Large . . . . 180 . . . ½ roll
French Rolls,
   Small . . . . 130 . . . "
Golden Twist . . . 110 . . . each
Hamburger . . . . . 110 . . . "
Hearth . . . . 60 . . . "
Old-Fashioned . . 37 . . . "
Parkerhouse . . . . 57 . . . "
Party Pan . . . . . . 35 . . . "
Sandwich . . . . . . 140 . . . each
Sesame Crisp . . . 70 . . . each

CARNATION COMPANY

Evaporated
   Milk . . . . 565 . . . 13 fl. oz. can
Instant Nonfat
   Dry Milk . . . . . 80 . . . 8 oz. recon-
                              stituted
Instant Natural
   Flavor Malted
   Milk . . . . 90 . . . 3 heaping
                              tsps.
Instant Chocolate
   Flavor Malted
   Milk . . . . 85 . . . "
Instant
   Breakfast . . . . 290 . . . 8 oz. serving
Coffee-Mate . . . . 10 . . . 1 tsp.

THE CHUN KING CORPORATION

Fortune Cookies . . 125 . . 1 oz.
Chicken Divider-
   Pak Chow
   Mein . . . . 91 . . . 8 oz.
Beef Divider-Pak
   Chow Mein . . . 103 . . . 10 oz.
Mushroom
   Divider-Pak
   Chow Mein . . . 75 . . . 10 oz.
Krispi Meatless
   Chow Mein . . . 75 . . . 8 oz.
Subgum Chicken
   Chow Mein . . . 78 . . . "

Krispi Beef
   Chop Suey . . . 122 . . . 8 ozs.
Krispi Chicken
   Chow Mein . . . 111 . . . "
Chop Suey
   Vegetables . . . 29 . . . 1 lb. can
Chinese
   Vegetables . . . 39 . . . "
Bean Sprouts . . . 39 . . . "
Chow Mein
   Noodles . . . . . 141 . . . 1 oz.
Chow Mein
   Noodles . . . . . 424 . . . 3 oz. can
3 lb. Meatless
   Chow Mein . . . 83 . . . 8 oz. serving
3 lb. Meatless
   Chow Mein . . . 499 . . . 3 lb. can
3 lb. Chicken
   Chow Mein . . . 100 . . . 8 oz. serving
3 lb. Chicken
   Chow Mein . . . 600 . . . 3 lb. can
3 lb. Beef
   Chop Suey . . . 150 . . . 8 oz. serving
3 lb. Beef
   Chop Suey . . . . 898 . . . 3 lb. can
Frozen Egg Foo
   Young . . . . 242 . . . 12 oz. pkg.
Frozen Chicken
   Cantonese
   Dinner . . . . 302 . . . 11 oz. pkg.
      Egg Rolls . . 93 . . .
      Rice . . . . . . 78 . . .
      Chow Mein . . 131 . . .

Frozen Shrimp
   Chow Mein . . . 198 . . . per 16 oz.
                     tray
Frozen Pork
   Fried Rice . . . 396 . . . per 10 oz.
                     tray
Frozen Beef
   Chop Suey . . . 252 . . . per 16 oz.
                     tray
Jeno's
   Plain Pizza . . . 990 . . . total pkg.
      Sauce . . . . . 168 . . . 8½ oz. can
      Yeast . . . . . 14 . . . 5 grams
      Cheese . . . . 84 . . . ¾ oz.
      Flour Mix . . 720 . . . 6½ oz.

CROSSE & BLACKWELL PRODUCTS

Apricot
   Preserves .... 67...Approx.
                       1 tbsp.
Blackberry
   Preserves .... 71...   "
Black Currant
   Preserves .... 71...   "
Cherry
   Preserves .... 69...   "
Damson
   Preserves .... 66...   "
Grape
   Preserves .... 70...   "
Peach
   Preserves .... 68...   "
Pineapple
   Preserves .... 72...   "
Raspberry
   Preserves .... 71...   "
Strawberry
   Preserves .... 71...   "
Orange
   Marmalade
   (English
   Style) .... 70...   "
Sweet Orange
   Marmalade ... 71...   "
Apple Jelly ..... 68...   "
Blackberry
   Apple Jelly ... 68...   "
Blackberry Jelly .. 67...   "
Cherry Jelly .... 69...   "
Crabapple Jelly .. 68...   "
Damson Jelly ... 67...   "
Grape Jelly ..... 69...   "
Guava Jelly ..... 72...   "
Mint Jelly ...... 67...   "
Quince Jelly .... 68...   "
Red Currant .... 66...   "
Strawberry ..... 68...   "
Date & Nut
   Roll ....230...Scant 4 oz.
Chocolate
   Nut Roll .....230...   "

Fruit &
   Nut Roll .....270...Scant 4 oz.
Brown Bread ...186...   "
Plum Pudding ...300...   "

Black
   Bean Soup ...104...Scant 1 cup
Consomme Madri-
   lene—Clear .. 40...   "
Consomme Madri-
   lene—Red .... 32...   "
Crab Soup ..... 64...   "
Lobster Soup
   (Creamed) ... 96...   "
Cream of
   Onion Soup ... 80...   "
Cream of
   Shrimp Soup ..102...   "
French
   Onion Soup ... 50...   "
Mushroom
   Bisque ......112...   "
Vichyssoise ....102...   "
Scotch Broth .... 86...   "

Chili Con Carne ..254...   "
Corned Beef
   Hash ....378...   "
Lamb Stew .....150...   "

C & B Steak
   Sauce .... 26...Approx.
                       1 tbsp.
Mint Sauce .... 28...   "
Worcestershire
   Sauce .... 27...   "
Seafood Cocktail
   Sauce .... 32...   "

DIET DELIGHT

Apple Jelly ..... 4...1 tsp.
Applesauce ..... 50...½ cup
Apricots .... 60...   "
Apricot Pineapple
   Preserves .... 4...1 tsp.

Asparagus	14	½ cup
Green Beans	20	"
Seedless Black-berry Jam	4	1 tsp.
Royal Anne Cherries	60	½ cup
Chocolate Topping	16	1 tsp.
Corn	70	½ cup
Fruit Cocktail	60	"
Fruit Salad	60	"
French Dressing	4	1 tsp.
Concord Grape Jelly	4	"
Grapefruit Juice	60	6 fl. oz.
Grapefruit Segments	45	½ cup
Italian Dressing	4	1 tsp.
Mandarin Oranges	45	½ cup
Orange Marmalade	4	1 tsp.
Pancake Syrup	16	1 tbsp.
Cling Peaches, Halves	50	½ cup
Cling Peaches, Slices	50	"
Freestone Peaches, Halves	50	"
Freestone Peaches, Slices	50	"
Pears	60	"
Peas	50	"
Peas & Carrots	40	"
Pineapple, Chunks, Crushed, Tidbits, Slices	70	"
Raspberry Jam	4	1 tsp.
Strawberry Jam	4	"
Thousand Island Dressing	6	"
Tomatoes	25	½ cup
Tomato Juice	35	6 fl. oz.
Whipped Dressing —Mayo-lite	10	1 tsp.
Purple Plums	70	½ cup

DROMEDARY
(National Biscuit Company)

Banana Nut Roll	71	½" slice
Chocolate Nut Roll	87	"
Date Nut Roll	75	"
Orange Nut Roll	77	"
Corn Bread Mix	123	1" x 4" piece
Corn Muffin Mix	192	medium sized
Cup Cake Mix	129	1 cup cake
Date Muffin Mix	183	medium sized
Fudge & Frosting Mix	55	1" x 1" x ½" piece
Gingerbread Mix	100	1" x 4" piece
Pound Cake Mix	278	1" slice
Dromedary Chopped Dates	493	1 cup lightly packed
Dromedary Fruits and Peels	765	8 oz. pkg.
Dromedary Pimientos	15	2 oz. jar
Pimientos	54	7 oz. tin
Dromedary Pitted Dates	470	1 cup lightly packed

EMPIRE STATE PICKLING CO.

Sliver Floss Sauerkraut	39	1 cup

FAIRMONT FOOD COMPANY

Buttermilk	118	8 oz.
Chocolate Drink	152	"

Chocolate Milk ..213... 8 oz.
Fortified
   Skim Milk ....112... "
Homogenized Vita-
   min D Milk ...158... "
Skim Milk ...... 97... "
Coffee Cream ... 57...2 tbsp.
Half and Half ... 80...¼ cup
Sour Cream .... 57...2 tbsp.
Whipping
   Cream ...... 68...2 tbsp. after
                whipping

Cream Cheese ..101...1 oz.
Creamed Cottage
   Cheese ...... 73...⅓ cup
Dry Curd Cottage
   Cheese
   (unsalted) .... 44... "
Neufchatel ..... 74...1 oz.

Ice Cream,
   Vanilla ......138...½ cup
Ice Cream,
   Chocolate ....149... "
Ice Cream,
   Strawberry ...136... "
Deluxe Ice Cream,
   French
   Vanilla ......173... "
Dairyfair,
   Vanilla ......108... "
Dairyfair,
   Strawberry ...115... "
Sherbet
   (Orange) .....122... "
Eskimo Pies,
   Chocolate or
   Almond
   Covered .....188...3 oz.
Eskimo Pies,
   Fudge Ice
   Milk ....165... "
Fudgsicle ......109... "
Popsicle .... 73... "
Fruit Drink
   (Orange) .....121...8 oz.

R.T. FRENCH COMPANY

Worcestershire
   Sauce .... 6...1 tbsp.
Barbecue Sauce
   (Mild) ...... 17... "
Barbecue Sauce
   (Regular) .... 9... "
Barbecue Sauce
   (Smoky) ..... 15... "
Brown & Spicy
   Mustard ..... 17... "
Cream Salad
   Mustard ..... 11... "
Medford
   Mustard ..... 15... "
Mustard with
   Horseradish .. 17... "
Mustard with
   Onion .... 21... "
Ring Star
   Mustard ..... 12... "

Potato Products
Idaho Mashed
   Potato (pre-
   pared with
   milk and
   butter) ......114...½ cup
Country Style
   Mashed Potato
   Flakes (pre-
   pared with
   milk and
   butter) ......137... "
Potato Pancake
   Mix (prepared
   with egg) .... 30...1 small pan-
                cake
Scalloped Potatoes
   (prepared with
   butter) ......109...½ cup
Potatoes Au
   Gratin .... 95... "

Envelope Pack Line
Au Jus Gravy .... 5...¼ cup
Brown Gravy .... 18... "

Chicken Gravy ... 32 ... ¼ cup
Mushroom
    Gravy .... 16 ...   "
Onion Gravy .... 18 ...   "
Gravy for Pork ... 19 ... ¼ cup
Gravy for Turkey .. 23 ...   "
Cheese Sauce ... 81 ...   "
Hollandaise
    Sauce .... 16 ... 1 tbsp.
Pizza Sauce .... 18 ... 2 tbsp.
Sour Cream
    Sauce .... 25 ... 1 tbsp.
Spaghetti Sauce—
    Italian .... 112 ... ⅝ cup
Spaghetti Sauce
  with
    Mushrooms ... 91 ...   "
Stroganoff
    Sauce .... 104 ... ⅓ cup
Beef Stew
    Seasoning .... 133 ... package
Chili-O .... 123 ...   "
Ground Beef
  Seasoning with
    Onions ...... 79 ...   "
Sloppy Joes
    Seasoning .... 117 ...   "
Taco Seasoning .. 123 ...   "

Spices and Spice Blends
Bacon, Imitation
    Crumbles .... 7 ... 1 tsp.
Barbecue
    Seasoning .... 7 ...   "
Beef Flavor
    Stock Base ... 9 ...   "
Celery .... 2 ...   "
Chicken Flavor
    Stock Base ... 8 ...   "
Cinnamon
    Sugar .... 15 ...   "
Garlic Salt ...... 4 ...   "
Garlic Salt,
    Parslied ..... 6 ...   "
Hickory Smoke
    Salt .... 1 ... 1 tsp.
Lemon & Pepper
    Seasoning .... 5 ...   "

Meat Tenderizer .. 2 ... 1 tsp.
Meat Tenderizer
  (Seasoned) ... 2 ...   "
Onion Salt ..... 5 ...   "
Pepper,
  Seasoned .... 7 ...   "
Pizza Seasoning .. 4 ...   "
Salad Lift ...... 6 ...   "
Salt, Imit. Butter
  Flavor .... 8 ...   "
Seafood
  Seasoning .... 2 ...   "
Seasoning Salt ... 3 ...   "

Extracts
Almond, Pure
  Extract ...... 12 ...   "
Anise, Pure
  Extract ...... 26 ...   "
Banana, Imitation
  Extract ...... 20 ...   "
Black Walnut,
  Imitation
  Flavor .... 12 ...   "
Brandy, Pure
  Flavor .... 16 ...   "
Butter, Imitation
  Flavor .... 8 ...   "
Cherry, Imitation
  Extract ...... 16 ...   "
Coconut, Imitation
  Flavor .... 17 ...   "
Lemon, Pure
  Extract ...... 30 ...   "
Maple, Imitation
  Flavor .... 9 ...   "
Orange, Pure
  Extract ...... 30 ...   "
Peach, Imitation
  Extract ...... 23 ... 1 tsp.
Peppermint, Pure
  Extract ...... 24 ...   "
Pineapple, Imitation
  Extract ...... 14 ...   "
Raspberry, Imitation
  Extract ...... 14 ...   "
Rum, Pure
  Flavor .... 19 ...   "

Sherry, Pure
Flavor . . . . 17 . . . 1 tsp.
Strawberry,
Imitation
Extract . . . . . . 16 . . . "
Vanilla, (Clear)
Imitation . . . . . 12 . . . "
Vanilla, Pure
Extract . . . . . . 13 . . . "
Wintergreen, Pure
Extract . . . . . . 24 . . . "

GENERAL FOODS
**(Baker's, Birds Eye, Log Cabin,
Roast 'n Boast, Shake 'n Bake, Post,
Good Seasons, Jell-O, D-Zerta,
Maxwell House, Swans Down, Tang)**

BAKER'S
German Sweet
Chocolate . . . . 141 . . . 4½ squares
Semi-Sweet
Chocolate . . . . 132 . . . 1 square
Semi-Sweet
Chocolate
Chips . . . . 191 . . . ¼ cup
Unsweetened
Chocolate . . . . 136 . . . 1 square
Angel Flake
Coconut . . . . . 89 . . . ¼ cup
Coconut
Crunchies . . . . 176 . . . "
Premium Shred
Coconut . . . . . 105 . . . "
Cookie Coconut . . 140 . . . "
Southern Style
Coconut . . . . . 85 . . . "

BIRDS EYE
Dessert Products
Cool 'n Creamy
Pudding
(average of
flavors) . . . . . . 178 . . . ½ cup
Cool Whip
Whipped
Topping . . . . . 14 . . . 1 tbsp.

Fruits
Blueberries,
Quick Thaw . . . 110 . . . ½ cup
Mixed Fruit,
Quick Thaw . . . 130 . . . "
Red Raspberries,
Quick Thaw . . . 140 . . . "
Sliced Peaches,
Quick Thaw . . . 130 . . . "
Strawberries,
Quick Thaw . . . 110 . . . "
Strawberries,
Whole . . . . 80 . . . ¼ pkg.
Strawberry
Halves . . . . . . 170 . . . ½ cup
Sweet Cherries,
Quick Thaw . . . 120 . . . "

Regular Vegetables
Baby Butter
Beans . . . . 130 . . . ⅓ pkg.
Collard Greens,
Chopped . . . . . 30 . . . "
Corn on Cob . . . . 130 . . . 1 ear
Kale, Chopped . . . 30 . . . ½ cup
Mustard Greens,
Chopped . . . . . 18 . . . "
Okra, Cut . . . . . . 25 . . . "
Okra, Whole . . . . 35 . . . "
Onion Rings,
French Fried . . 166 . . . 2 ozs.
Onions,
Chopped . . . . . 8 . . . ¼ cup
Onions, Small
Whole . . . . 40 . . . ½ cup
Peas, Black-Eye . . 120 . . . "
Squash, Cooked . . 50 . . . ⅓ pkg.
Sweet Potatoes,
Candied . . . . . 215 . . . "
Turnip Greens-
Chopped . . . . . 20 . . . ½ cup

5 Minute Vegetables
Asparagus, Cut . . 25 . . . ½ cup
Asparagus
Spears . . . . . . 25 . . . ⅓ pkg.
Broccoli,
Chopped . . . . . 25 . . . "

Broccoli Spears . . 25 . . . ⅓ pkg.
Cauliflower . . . . . 25 . . .   "
Corn, Sweet
   Whole Kernel . . 70 . . . ½ cup
Green Beans,
   Cut . . . . 25 . . . ⅓ pkg.
Green Beans,
   French Style . . 30 . . .   "
Green Beans,
   Italian . . . . . . 30 . . .   "
Lima Beans,
   Baby . . . . 120 . . . ½ cup
Lima Beans,
   Fordhook . . . . 100 . . . ⅓ pkg.
Mixed
   Vegetables . . . 60 . . . ½ cup
Peas, Sweet
   Green . . . . . . 70 . . .   "
Peas and
   Carrots . . . . . 50 . . .   "
Spinach,
   Chopped . . . . 20 . . . ⅓ pkg.
Spinach, Leaf . . . 20 . . .   "
Succotash . . . . . . 80 . . . ½ cup
Summer Squash,
   Sliced . . . . . . 18 . . .   "
Wax Beans, Cut . . 30 . . . ⅓ pkg.
Zucchini
   Squash . . . . . . 16 . . .   "

Deluxe Vegetables
Artichoke
   Hearts . . . . . . 20 . . . 5 or 6
Broccoli Spears,
   Baby . . . . 25 . . . ⅓ pkg.
Brussels Sprouts,
   Baby . . . . 35 . . . ½ cup
Corn, Sweet
   White . . . . . . 110 . . .   "
Green Beans,
   Whole . . . . . . 25 . . . ⅓ pkg.
Lima Beans,
   Tiny . . . . 120 . . . ½ cup
Peas, Tender Tiny . . 60 . . .   "

Combination Vegetables
Asparagus Spears
   w/Hollandaise
   Sauce . . . . 100 . . . ⅓ pkg.

Broccoli Spears
   w/Hollandaise
   Sauce . . . . 100 . . . ⅓ pkg.
Carrots w/Brown
   Sugar Glaze . . 80 . . . ½ cup
Corn and Peas
   w/Tomatoes . . 60 . . . ⅓ pkg.
Creamed
   Spinach . . . . . 60 . . .   "
French Green
   Beans w/Sliced
   Mushrooms . . . 30 . . .   "
French Green
   Beans
   w/Toasted
   Almonds . . . . . 50 . . . ½ cup

Green Peas and
   Celery . . . . . . 45 . . .   "
Green Peas and
   Pearl Onions . . 60 . . . ⅓ pkg.
Green Peas and
   Potatoes
   w/Cream
   Sauce . . . . 120 . . .   "
Green Peas
   w/Cream
   Sauce . . . . 120 . . .   "
Green Peas
   w/Sliced
   Mushrooms . . . 70 . . .   "
Mixed Vegetables
   w/Onion
   Sauce . . . . 110 . . . ½ cup
Rice and Peas w/
   Mushrooms . . . 110 . . . ⅓ pkg.
Sliced Beets
   w/Orange
   Flavor Glaze . . 50 . . .   "
Small Onions
   w/Cream
   Sauce . . . . 110 . . .   "
Sweet Potatoes
   w/Brown Sugar
   Pineapple
   Glaze . . . . 140 . . . ½ cup
Vegetable
   Jubilee . . . . . . 120 . . . ⅓ pkg.

International Vegetables

Bavarian Style
Beans and
Spaetzle .....110...⅓ pkg.
Chinese Style
Vegetables ... 70... "
Danish Style
Vegetables ... 80... "
Hawaiian Style
Vegetables ... 90... "
Italian Style
Vegetables ... 90... "
Japanese Style
Vegetables ... 90...⅓ pkg.
Mexican Style
Vegetables ...120... "
Parisian Style
Vegetables ... 90... "
Spanish Style
Vegetable
Medley ...... 70... "

LOG CABIN SYRUPS

Regular syrup ... 46...1 tbsp.
Buttered
Syrup .... 52... "
Country Kitchen
Pancake and
Waffle Syrup .. 51... "
Maple-Honey
Syrup .... 54... "

OPEN PIT BARBECUE SAUCES

Original Flavor .. 26...1 tbsp.
Original Flavor
with Minced
Onions ...... 27... "
Hickory Smoke
Flavor .... 27... "
Hot 'n Spicy .... 27... "

ROAST 'n BOAST OVEN COOKING BAG AND SAUCE MIXES

For Beef ....129...1 env.
For Chicken .....119... "
For Pork ....145... "
For Stew ....126... "

SHAKE 'n BAKE SEASONED COATING MIXES

For Chicken ....276...1 env.
For Fish ......224... "
For Hamburger ..158... "
For Pork ......260... "

POST CEREALS

Alpha-Bits Sugar
Frosted Oat
Cereal ....110...1 cup
Crispy Critters
Oat Cereal ....110... "
Fortified Oat
Flakes ....110...⅔ cup
40% Bran
Flakes ....100... "
Frosted Rice
Krinkles
Cereal ....110...⅞ cup
Grape-Nuts Brand
Cereal ....100...¼ cup
Grape-Nuts
Flakes ....100...⅔ cup
Honeycomb Sweet
Crisp Corn
Cereal ....110...1⅓ cups

Pebbles, Cocoa ..110...⅞ cup
Pebbles, Fruity ..110... "
Pink Panther
Flakes ......112...⅔ cup
Post Toasties
Corn Flakes ...110...1 cup
Raisin Bran .....100...½ cup
Raisin Bran,
Cinnamon .... 92... "
Super Orange
Crisp Honey-
Flavored
Wheat Puffs
w/Orange-
Flavored
Cereal Rings ..109...1 cup
Super Sugar Crisp
Wheat Puffs ..110...⅞ cup

BIRDS EYE CONCENTRATES
(Prepared as Directed on Package)

Birds Eye Concentrated Orange Juice .... 51 ...½ cup
Awake Frozen Concentrate for Imitation Orange Juice .. 55... "
Orange Plus Frozen Concentrate for Imitation Orange Juice .. 67... "
Thick & Frosty Frozen Thick Shake Concentrate (Avg. for all flavors) ....314...1 cup
Dream Whip Whipped Topping Mix ..... 10...1 tbsp.

D-ZERTA BRAND DESSERTS

D-Zerta Gelatin (avg. for all flavors) ...... 8 ...½ cup
Butterscotch and Vanilla Puddings (avg. for both w/whole milk) ....108... "
(avg. for both w/nonfat milk) .... 70... "
Chocolate Pudding (made with whole milk) ...105... "
(made with nonfat milk) .. 70... "
Whipped Topping Mix .... 8 ...1 tbsp.

GOOD SEASONS SALAD DRESSING MIXES

Mild Italian, Cheese Italian and Bleu Cheese (avg. of all) .... 89 ...1 tbsp.
Garlic, Italian, Onion, and Cheese Garlic (avg. of all) ... 84... "
Old Fashion French ...... 83... "
Riviera French .. 90... "
Thick 'N Creamy Bleu Cheese .. 96... "
Thick 'N Creamy French ...... 97... "
Thick 'N Creamy Italian .... 94... "
Thick 'N Creamy Thousand Island .... 80... "

JELL-O BRAND DESSERTS

Cheesecake ....260...⅛ cake
Gelatin (avg. for regular flavors) ...... 80...½ cup
Gelatin (avg. for wild flavors) ...... 80... "
Golden Egg Custard (w/whole milk— no egg yolk) ...170... "
(w/nonfat milk—no egg yolk) .....135... "
Instant Puddings & Pie Fillings: Banana, Butterscotch, Fr. Vanilla, Lemon, Pineapple, and Vanilla (Avg. for all) ....180...½ cup

Chocolate and
Chocolate
Fudge .... 190 ... ½ cup
Coconut
Cream .... 190 ...   "
Puddings & Pie
Fillings: Butter-
scotch, Fr.
Vanilla, Vanilla
(avg. w/whole
milk) .... 177 ...   "
Chocolate,
Chocolate
Fudge, Milk
Chocolate
(avg. w/whole
milk) .... 183 ...   "
Coconut Cream
Pie (w/whole
milk) .... 120 ... ⅙ of pie
Tapioca Puddings
(avg. all
flavors) ...... 170 ... ½ cup
Whip 'n Chill
Dessert: Lemon,
Strawberry,
and Vanilla
(avg. w/whole
milk) .... 140 ...   "
Chocolate
(w/whole
milk) .... 150 ...   "

OTHER GENERAL FOODS PRODUCTS
Kool-Aid Soft
Drink Mix,
regular (avg. for
all flavors) .... 100 ... 1 cup
Kool-Aid Sugar
Sweetened
Drink Mix
(avg. for all
flavors) ...... 90 ...   "

Maxwell House,
Sanka Brand,
and Yuban
coffees,
ground ..... 2 ... 6 fl. oz.

Instant Maxwell
House, Sanka
Brand, and
Yuban
coffees ...... 4 ... 6 fl. oz.
Maxim Freeze-
Dried Coffee .. 4 ...   "
Sanka Brand
Freeze-Dried
Coffee .... 4 ...   "
Max-Pax Coffee
Rings .... 2 ...   "

Minute Rice
(no butter or
salt) .... 120 ... ⅔ cup
Minute Rice
Drumstick
Mix .... 170 ... ½ cup
Minute Rice
Rib Roast
Mix .... 150 ... ½ cup
Minute Rice
Spanish Rice
Mix .... 150 ...   "
Minute Tapioca
(fluffy pudding
recipe) ...... 150 ...   "
(dry product) .. 40 ... 1 tbsp.
Postum Cereal
Beverage,
Instant ...... 12 ... 1 cup
Start Instant
Breakfast
Drink .... 60 ... ½ cup

Swans Down
Angel Food
Cake Mix .... 140 ... ¹⁄₁₂ cake
Swans Down
Devil's Food
Cake Mix .... 180 ...   "
Swans Down
Yellow Cake
Mix .... 180 ...   "

Tang Instant
Breakfast Drinks
Orange, Grape,
Grapefruit .... 50 ... ½ cup

GERBER BABY FOODS

Strained Baby Foods
Beef .... 97...per container
Beef with Beef
   Heart .... 99...   "
Beef Liver ...... 94...   "
Chicken .... 151...   "
Egg Yolks ......204...   "
Egg Yolks and
   Ham ....196...   "
Ham ....123...   "
Lamb ....104...   "
Pork ....117...   "
Turkey ....132...per container
Veal .... 98...   "
Beef with
   Vegetables ...105...   "
Chicken with
   Vegetables ...101...   "
Ham with Vege-
   tables ....109...   "
Turkey with
   Vegetables ... 96...   "
Veal with
   Vegetables ... 81...   "

Creamed Cottage
   Cheese with
     Pineapple ....181...   "

Beets .... 55...   "
Carrots .... 36...   "
Creamed Corn ... 81...   "
Creamed
   Spinach ..... 51...   "
Garden
   Vegetables ... 44...   "
Green Beans .... 32...   "
Mixed
   Vegetables ... 52...   "
Peas .... 60...   "
Squash .... 32...   "
Sweet Potatoes .. 98...   "

Beef and Egg
   Noodles ..... 60...   "
Cereal, Egg Yolks
   and Bacon .... 93...   "

Vegetables and
   Lamb .... 68...per container
Vegetables and
   Liver with
     Bacon ...... 76...   "
Vegetables and
   Turkey ...... 49...   "

Applesauce ..... 117...   "
Applesauce and
   Apricots ....121...   "
Applesauce with
   Pineapple ....103...   "
Apricots with
   Tapioca ......110...   "
Bananas ....114...   "
Bananas with
   Pineapple and
   Tapioca ......110...   "
Dutch Apple
   Dessert ......141...   "
Fruit Dessert ....121...   "
Peaches ....117...   "
Pears .... 91...   "
Pears and
   Pineapple .... 98...   "
Plums with
   Tapioca ......127...   "
Prunes with
   Tapioca ......119...   "

Chicken Noodle
   Dinner ...... 58...   "
Cream of Chicken
   Soup .... 79...   "
Macaroni, Tomato,
   Beef and
     Bacon .... 78...   "
Vegetables and
   Bacon .... 95...   "
Vegetables and
   Beef .... 77...   "
Vegetables and
   Chicken ..... 56...   "
Vegetables and
   Ham with
     Bacon ...... 93...   "

Cherry Vanilla
   Pudding .....143... per container
Chocolate Flavored
   Custard
   Pudding ....123...   "
Orange Pudding ..125...   "
Vanilla Custard
   Pudding .....123...   "

Apple Juice ..... 60...   "
Apple-Cherry
   Juice .... 69...   "
Mixed Fruit
   Juice .... 66...   "
Orange Juice .... 60...   "
Orange-Apple
   Juice Drink ... 67...per container
Orange-Apple-
   Banana
   Juice .... 81...   "
Orange-Apricot
   Juice .... 83...   "
Orange-Pineapple
   Juice .... 62...   "
Pineapple-Grape-
   fruit Juice
   Drink .... 72...   "
Prune-Orange
   Juice .... 92...   "

Barley Cereal,
   dry .... 26...3 tbsp.
High Protein
   Cereal, dry ... 26...   "
Mixed Cereal,
   dry .... 27...   "
Oatmeal, dry .... 28...   "
Rice Cereal,
   dry .... 26...   "

Mixed Cereal with
   Applesauce and
   Bananas .....109...per container
Oatmeal with
   Applesauce and
   Bananas .....103...   "
Rice Cereal with
   Applesauce and
   Bananas ..... 92...   "

Teething
   Biscuits ..... 43...each
Animal Shaped
   Cookies ...... 28...   "

Junior Foods
Beef and Egg
   Noodles .....102...per container
Cereal, Egg Yolks
   and Bacon ....159...   "
Chicken Noodle
   Dinner ...... 95...   "
Cream of Chicken
   Soup ....131...   "
Macaroni, Tomato,
   Beef and
   Bacon ....140...   "
Spaghetti, Tomato
   Sauce and
   Beef ....138...per container
Split Peas with
   Bacon ....170...   "
Vegetables and
   Bacon ....134...   "
Vegetables and
   Beef ....119...   "
Vegetables and
   Chicken .....108...   "
Vegetables and
   Ham with
   Bacon ....121...   "
Vegetables and
   Lamb ....117...   "
Vegetables and
   Liver with
   Bacon ....102...   "
Vegetables and
   Turkey ...... 83...   "

Applesauce .....180...   "
Applesauce and
   Apricots .....187...   "
Applesauce with
   Pineapple ....167...   "
Apricots with
   Tapioca .....180...   "

Bananas with
   Pineapple and
   Tapioca .....185...per container
Dutch Apple
   Dessert ......231...   "
Fruit Dessert ....185...   "
Peaches ....176...   "
Pears ....139...   "
Pears and
   Pineapple ....154...   "
Plums with
   Tapioca ......225...   "
Prunes
   w/Tapioca ...202...   "

Banana
   Pudding .....202...   "
Cherry Vanilla
   Pudding .....235...   "
Chocolate Flavored
   Custard
   Pudding .....207...per container
Vanilla Custard
   Pudding .....197...   "

Carrots .... 61...   "
Creamed Corn ...146...   "
Creamed Green
   Beans with
   Bacon ....146...   "
Creamed
   Spinach ..... 87...   "
Mixed
   Vegetables ... 83...   "
Squash .... 53...   "
Sweet Potatoes ..156...   "

Beef with
   Vegetables ...108...4½ oz. jar
Chicken with
   Vegetables ...111...   "
Ham with
   Vegetables ... 99...   "
Turkey with
   Vegetables ... 93...   "
Veal with
   Vegetables ... 82...   "

Beef ....107...per container
Chicken ....153...   "
Chicken Sticks ..212...   "
Lamb .... 99...   "
Meat Sticks ....156...   "
Pork ....124...   "
Veal ....103...   "

GOODMAN'S

Goodman's
   Matzos ......105...1 oz.
Goodman's
   Noodles .....110...1 oz.,
                    uncooked
Goodman's
   Spaghetti &
   Macaroni ....105...   "

THE GORTON CORPORATION

Frozen Flounder
   fillets ...... 20...per oz.
Frozen Cod
   fillets ...... 19...   "
Frozen Haddock
   fillets ...... 20...   "
Frozen Perch
   fillets ...... 28...   "
Frozen Whiting
   fillets ...... 22...   "
Frozen Pollock
   fillets ...... 24...   "
Frozen Scallops.. 21...   "
Frozen Salmon
   steaks .... 63...   "
Frozen Clams ... 24...   "
Fish Roe
   (canned) ..... 17...   "
Fish Cake
   (canned) ..... 25...   "
Fish Flakes
   (canned) ..... 21...   "
Breaded
   Scallops ..... 27...   "
Breaded 1 oz.
   Cod portions .. 34...   "
Breaded 2 oz.
   Cod portions .. 27...   "   85

Breaded 4 oz.
Cod portions . . 30 . . . per oz.
Breaded Flounder
portions . . . . . 32 . . . "
Breaded Haddock
portions . . . . . 27 . . . "
Breaded Perch
portions . . . . . 37 . . . "
Breaded Whiting
portions . . . . . 35 . . . "
Fried
Portions . . . . 43-54 . . . "
Fish Puffs . . . . . . 83 . . . "
Crispy Crunchy
Fish Sticks . . . 82 . . . "
Fillet of Sole in
Lemon Butter
Sauce . . . . 45 . . . "
Scallops in Lemon
Butter Sauce . . 56 . . . "
Shrimp Scampi . . 79 . . . "
Flounder
Almondine . . . 53 . . . "
Fish Sticks
(cooked) . . . . . 52 . . . "
Haddock Sticks
(cooked) . . . . . 53 . . . "
Scallops
(cooked) . . . . . 54 . . . "
Fish Cakes
(cooked) . . . . . 60 . . . "
Shrimp
(cooked) . . . . . 67 . . . "
Fish & Chips
(cooked) . . . . . 126 . . . "

GREEN GIANT COMPANY

Canned

Asparagus . . . . . . 40 . . . 1 cup
Green Beans . . . . 40 . . . "
Three Bean
Salad . . . . 180 . . . "
Golden Cream
Style Corn . . . . 230 . . . "
Golden Whole
Kernel Corn . . 170 . . . "

White Whole
Kernel Corn . . 150 . . . 1 cup
Tiny Golden Whole
Kernel Corn . . 170 . . . "
Mexicorn . . . . . . 150 . . . "
Niblets Golden
Whole Kernel
Corn . . . . 150 . . . "
Brown Gravy . . . . 33 . . . 3½ ozs.
Mushroom Steak
Sauce . . . . 33 . . . "
Mushrooms . . . . . 15 . . . 2 oz.
Peas . . . . 130 . . . 1 cup
Peas with
Onions . . . . . . 130 . . . "

Frozen

Brussels Sprouts
in Butter
Sauce . . . . 120 . . . 1 cup
Lima Beans in
Butter Sauce . . 250 . . . "
Carrot Nuggets in
Butter Sauce . . 110 . . . "
Spinach in Butter
Sauce . . . . 90 . . . "
Asparagus in
Butter Sauce . . 90 . . . "
Green Beans in
Butter Sauce . . 80 . . . "
Mixed Vegetables
in Butter
Sauce . . . . 130 . . . "
White Corn in
Butter Sauce . . 190 . . . "
Peas in Butter
Sauce . . . . 170 . . . "
Peas with Onions
in Butter
Sauce . . . . 170 . . . "
Mushrooms in
Butter Sauce . . 35 . . . 2 ozs.
Broccoli in Butter
Sauce . . . . 100 . . . 1 cup
Mexicorn in
Butter Sauce . . 190 . . . "
Niblets Corn in
Butter Sauce . . 190 . . . "

Cauliflower in
   Cheese
   Sauce . . . . 170 . . . 1 cup
Broccoli in Cheese
   Sauce . . . . 150 . . .   "
Creamed
   Onions . . . . . 110 . . .   "
Creamed
   Spinach . . . . . 250 . . .   "
Cream Style
   Corn . . . . 180 . . .   "
Honey Glazed
   Carrots . . . . . . 190 . . .   "
Peas in Cream
   Sauce . . . . 160 . . .   "
Peas and Carrots
   in Cream
   Sauce . . . . 150 . . .   "
Green Beans &
   Onions in
   Sauce . . . . 80 . . .   "
Corn-on-the-
   Cob . . . . 170 . . . 1 ear
Brown Rice in
   Beef Stock . . . 300 . . . 1 cup
Long Grain White
   & Wild Rice . . . 250 . . .   "
Rice Medley . . . . 250 . . .   "
Rice Pilaf . . . . . . 250 . . .   "
Rice Verdi . . . . . . 300 . . .   "
Broccoli
   Casserole . . . . 270 . . .   "
Brussels Sprouts
   Casserole . . . . 180 . . .   "
Spinach
   Casserole . . . . 170 . . .   "
Green Bean
   Casserole . . . . 110 . . .   "
Cauliflower
   Casserole . . . . 180 . . .   "
Scalloped Corn
   Casserole . . . . 370 . . .   "
Stuffed Baked
   Potatoes with
   Cheese . . . . . . 340 . . . 6 ozs.
Stuffed Baked
   Potatoes with
   Sour Cream . . 340 . . .   "

HERSHEY FOODS

Baking
   Chocolate . . . . 190 . . . 1 oz.
Chocolate
   Flavored
   Syrup . . . . 70 . . . 2 tbsp.
Cocoa . . . . 120 . . . ⅓ cup
Hershey-ets . . . . 140 . . . 34 pieces
Hot Cocoa
   Mix . . . . 110 . . . 1 oz.
Instant Cocoa
   Mix . . . . 80 . . . 3 tbsp.
Kisses . . . . 160 . . . 6 pieces
Krackel . . . . 210 . . . 1.4 ozs.
Milk Chocolate . . 220 . . .   "
Milk Chocolate
   with Almonds . . 200 . . . 1.3 ozs.
Milk Chocolate
   Chips . . . . 240 . . . ¼ cup
Milk Chocolate
   Fudge
   Topping . . . . . 100 . . . 2 tbsp.
Mini Chips . . . . . 220 . . . ¼ cup
Mr. Goodbar . . . . 280 . . . 1.8 ozs.
Rally . . . . 260 . . .   "
Reese's Peanut
   Butter Cups . . 270 . . . 2 cups
Semi Sweet Choc-
   olate Chips . . . 220 . . . ¼ cup
Special Dark . . . . 220 . . . 1.4 ozs.

HORMEL CANNED MEATS

Dinty Moore Beef
   Stew . . . . 22 . . . 1 oz.
Dinty Moore Beef
   Stew . . . . 192 . . . 8½ oz. can
Dinty Moore Beef
   Stew . . . . 307 . . . 15 oz. can
Dinty Moore Beef
   Stew . . . . 531 . . . 24 oz. can
Beef, Chopped . . 72 . . . 1 oz.
Beef, Chopped . . 865 . . . 12 oz. can
Beef Stroganoff . . 40 . . . 1 oz.
Beef Stroganoff . . 643 . . . 16 oz. can
Breakfast
   Sausage . . . . . 105 . . . 1 oz.

Breakfast
    Sausage .....836...8 oz. can
Chili No Beans .. 52...1 oz.
Chili No Beans ..770...15 oz. can
Chili With
    Beans .... 34...1 oz.
Chili With
    Beans ......274...8 oz. can
Chili With
    Beans ......626...15 oz. can
Chili With
    Beans ......811...24 oz. can
Chili With
    Beans ......1400...40 oz. can
Chicken
    Cacciatori .... 24...1 oz.
Chicken
    Cacciatori ....386...16 oz. can
Frankfurters .... 81...1 oz.
Frankfurters ....965...12 oz. can
Garbanzo Soup .. 31...1 oz.
Garbanzo Soup ..461...15 oz. can
Ham, Canned ... 48...1 oz.
Ham, Canned ..1052...24 oz. can
Ham, Canned ..3072...4 lb. can
Ham, chopped .. 71...1 oz.
Ham, chopped ..852...8 oz. can
Ham, Deviled ... 73...1 oz.
Ham, Deviled ...219...3 oz. can
Hamburger,
    Braized ...... 48...1 oz.
Hamburger,
    Braized ......576...12 oz. can
Hash, Corned
    Beef .... 38...1 oz.
Hash, Corned
    Beef ....570...15 oz. can
Hash, Roast
    Beef .... 47...1 oz.
Hash, Roast
    Beef ....705...15 oz. can
Kottbullar ...... 48...1 oz.
Kottbullar ......773...1 lb. can
Liver Pate ...... 78...1 oz.
Liver Pate ......234...3 oz. can
Onion Soup .....145...15 oz. can
Picnic, Canned .. 52...1 oz.
Picnic, Canned ..208...¼ lb.

Pigs Feet ......440...1 pt.
Potted Meat ....169...3 oz. can
Spaghetti & Meat
    Balls .... 23...1 oz.
Spaghetti & Meat
    Balls ....347...15 oz. can
Spam .... 98...1 oz.
Spam ....1176...12 oz. can
Spam Spread ...216...3 oz. can
Tamales ...... 39...1 oz.
Tamales ......583...15 oz. can
Tongue .... 67...1 oz.
Tongue ....804...12 oz. can
Vienna Sausage.. 81...1 oz.
Vienna Sausage..324...4 oz. can

HUNT-WESSON FOODS

Apricots, whole
    unpeeled in
    heavy syrup .. 86...3½ oz.
Peaches, cling
    halves in
    heavy syrup .. 78...   "
Peaches, cling
    slices in heavy
    syrup .... 78...   "
Peaches, cling
    whole spiced, in
    extra heavy
    syrup .... 97...   "
Fruit Cocktail, in
    heavy syrup .. 76...   "
Pears, halves in
    heavy syrup .. 76...   "
Beans, Red, solids
    & liquid ...... 90...   "
Kidney Beans,
    solids &
    liquid .... 92...   "

White Beans with
    Pork & Tomato
    Sauce (Pork
    & Beans) .....150...   "
Hominy, white &
    yellow, solids
    & liquid ...... 69...   "

Potatoes, solids
   & liquid . . . . . . 44 . . . 3½ oz.
Spinach, leaf,
   solids &
   liquid . . . . 19 . . .   "
Tomatoes. . . . . . . 21 . . .   "
Tomato Juice . . . 19 . . .   "
Tomato Puree . . . 39 . . .   "
Tomato Paste . . . 82 . . .   "
Tomato Catsup . . 106 . . .   "
Tomato Sauce,
   regular . . . . . . 27 . . .   "
Tomato Sauce,
   with cheese &
   mushrooms . . 27 . . .   "
Chili Sauce . . . . . 104 . . .   "
Wesson Mayon-
   naise . . . . 718 . . .   "

KELLOGG'S

Corn Flakes . . . . 106 . . . 1⅓ cups
Pep . . . . 103 . . . ¾ cup
Rice Krispies . . . 108 . . . 1 cup
40% Bran
   Flakes . . . . . . 70 . . . ¾ cup
Raisin Bran . . . . . 101 . . .   "
Sugar Pops . . . . . 109 . . . 1 cup
Cocoa Krispies . . 111 . . . ¾ cup
Sugar Smacks . . 111 . . . 1 cup
Bran Buds . . . . . . 73 . . . ⅓ cup
All-Bran . . . . 64 . . . ½ cup
Sugar Frosted
   Flakes . . . . . . 108 . . . ¾ cup
Special K . . . . . . 107 . . . 1¼ cups
Froot Loops . . . . 115 . . . 1 cup
Product 19 . . . . 107 . . .   "
Concentrate . . . . 107 . . . ⅓ cup
Puffa Puffa
   Rice . . . . 120 . . . 1 cup
Frosted Mini-
   Wheats . . . . . . 107 . . . 4 biscuits
Apple Jacks . . . . 110 . . . 1 cup

KREY PACKING COMPANY

Sliced Beef &
   Gravy . . . . 32 . . . per oz.

Beef & Gravy . . . 54.5 . . . per oz.
Pork & Gravy . . . . 73 . . .   "
Beef Patties . . . . 54 . . .   "
Beef Stew . . . . . . 23 . . .   "
Stuffed
   Cabbage . . . . . 36 . . .   "
Stuffed Peppers . . 33 . . .   "
Corned Beef
   Hash . . . . 55 . . .   "

LA CHOY

Frozen Products

Fried Rice . . . . . 196 . . . 1 cup
Fried Rice with
   Meat . . . . 195 . . .   "
Vegetable Chow
   Mein . . . . 69 . . .   "
Chicken Chow
   Mein . . . . 202 . . .   "
Beef Chow
   Mein . . . . 113 . . .   "
Shrimp Chow
   Mein . . . . 79 . . .   "
Sweet & Sour
   Pork . . . . 272 . . .   "
Chow Mein
   Noodles . . . . . 129 . . . ½ cup
Soy Sauce . . . . . . 102 . . .   "
Egg Roll, Meat
   & Shrimp . . . . 141 . . . 2½ oz.
Egg Roll, Meat
   & Shrimp . . . . 55 . . . 1 oz.
Egg Roll, Meat
   & Shrimp . . . . 24 . . . 7/16 oz.
Egg Roll,
   Shrimp . . . . . . 24 . . . 7/16 oz.
Egg Roll,
   Chicken . . . . . 29 . . . 7/16 oz.
Egg Roll,
   Lobster . . . . . . 26 . . . 7/16 oz.
Shrimp Chow
   Mein Dinner . . 322 . . . entire dinner
Beef Chow Mein
   Dinner . . . . . . 343 . . .   "
Chicken Chow
   Mein Dinner . . 381 . . .   "

Canned Products
Chop Suey
   Vegetables ... 30...1 cup
Mixed Chinese
   Vegetables ... 22... "
Bean Sprouts ... 15... "
Chow Mein
   Noodles .....129...½ cup
Bamboo Shoots
   (sliced) ...... 6... "
Water Chestnuts
   (sliced) ...... 20... "
Soy Sauce ......102... "
Brown Sauce ....321...¼ cup
Shrimp Chow
   Mein Bi-Pack..110...1 cup
Beef Chow Mein
   Bi-Pack ...... 90... "
Chicken Chow
   Mein Bi-Pack..118... "
Mushroom Chow
   Mein Bi-Pack.. 81... "
Shrimp Chow
   Mein .... 75... "
Beef Chow
   Mein .... 77... "
Chicken Chow
   Mein .... 74... "
Meatless Chow
   Mein .... 49... "
Fried Rice ......137...½ cup
Sweet & Sour
   Sauce ......244... "

Skillet Dinners
Cantonese
   Seafood ..... 32...100 grams
Chicken Chow
   Mein .... 42... "
Egg Foo Young ..112... "
Pepper Steak ... 91... "
Sukiyaki ......110... "
Sweet & Sour ...139... "
Teriyaki ....133... "

THE LARSEN COMPANY
Pureed
   Asparagus .... 19...½ cup
Pureed Beets ... 35... "
Pureed Carrots .. 26... "
Pureed Golden
   Corn .... 79... "
Pureed Green
   Beans .... 27... "
Pureed Peas .... 48... "
Pureed Spinach .. 18... "
Pureed Golden
   Squash ...... 42... "
Veg-All Mixed
   Vegetables ... 45... "
Pureed
   Apricots .... 47... "
Pureed
   Peaches ..... 65... "
Pureed Pears ... 56... "

LIBBY, McNEILL & LIBBY

Canned Products
Beef Stew ...... 70...3½ ounces
Homestyle
   Hash ....200.... "
Meatball Stew ..120... "
Sloppy Joe
   Beef ....150... "
Sloppy Joe
   Pork ....150... "
Spaghetti &
   Meatballs .... 90... "
Vienna
   Sausage .....280... "
Carrots, diced or
   sliced .... 40...1 cup
Corn, Sweet,
   Cream Style ..180... "
Corn, Whole
   Kernel ......170... "
Peas ....115... "
Peas and
   Carrots ......100... "
Pumpkin .... 80... "
Sauerkraut ..... 45... "

Spinach	45	1 cup
Tomatoes, Stewed	60	"
Tomatoes, Whole Peeled	45	"
Beans, Deep Brown, Pork in Molasses Sauce	280	"
Beans, Deep Brown, Pork in Tomato Sauce	270	"
Beans, Deep Brown, Vegetarian in Tomato Sauce	260	"
Beans, Green, cut, French Style or Whole	40	"
Beans, Lima	160	"
Beans, Wax	40	"
Beets, Whole	65	"
Beets, Harvard	150	"
Beets, Pickled	160	"
Beets, Shoestring	50	"
Apricots, heavy syrup	200	"
Fruit Cocktail, heavy syrup	200	"
Fruits For Salad, heavy syrup	180	"
Peaches, Cling,	190	"
Pears	190	"
Pineapple, heavy syrup	190	"
Pineapple, Chunk or Crushed, juice pack	140	"
Pineapple, Sliced, juice pack	140	"
Pineapple Juice, un-sweetened	100	6 ounces
Tomato Juice	35	"

LIPTON, THOMAS J.

Lipton Soups

Beef Flavor Mushroom Mix	39	1 cup
Beef Flavor Noodle Soup with Vegetables	66	"
Chicken Noodle Soup with Diced White Chicken Meat	68	"
Chicken Rice Soup	62	"
Chicken Vegetable Soup	74	"
Country Vegetable Soup with Noodles	75	"
Green Pea Soup	138	"
Noodle Soup with Real Chicken Broth	53	"
Onion Soup and for California Dip	34	"
Potato Soup	100	"
Ring-O Noodle Soup with Real Chicken Broth	57	"
Tomato Vegetable Soup with Noodles	68	"
Vegetable Beef Soup	58	"
Italian Style Vegetable Soup with Spaghetti	103	"
Giggle Noodle Soup with Real Chicken Broth	76	"

Lipton Cup-a-Soup

Beef Flavor
    Noodle ...... 35 ...1 cup
Chicken Noodle
    with Chicken
    Meat .... 42 ...   "
Green Pea ......126 ...   "
Onion .... 30 ...   "
Tomato .... 80 ...   "
Chicken Flavor
    Cream Style .. 95 ...   "
Cream of
    Mushroom ... 86 ...   "
Chicken Flavored
    Broth .... 23 ...   "
Beef Flavored
    Broth .... 19 ...   "
Bean ....107 ...   "
Chicken
    Vegetable .... 41 ...   "
Cream of
    Tomato ...... 98 ...   "
Lentil ....119 ...   "
Lobster Bisque ..104 ...   "
New England
    Chowder .....102 ...   "
Noodle Soup
    Chicken
    Flavor .... 38 ...   "
Spring
    Vegetable .... 42 ...   "
Ring Noodle
    Chicken
    Flavor .... 55 ...   "

Wish-Bone Dressings

California
    Onion .... 76 ...1 tbsp.
Deluxe French .. 59 ...   "
Garlic French ... 66 ...   "
Green Goddess .. 68 ...   "
Italian .... 75 ...   "
Russian .... 54 ...   "
Thousand
    Island .... 71 ...   "
Creamy Onion ... 70 ...   "
Italian rosé ..... 58 ...   "

Chunky Blue
    Cheese ...... 74 ...1 tbsp.
Creamy Garlic ... 76 ...   "
Caesar .... 77 ...   "

Low Calorie Dressings

Low Calorie
    French
    Style .... 23 ...   "
Low Calorie
    Italian .... 16 ...   "
Low Calorie
    Russian ..... 24 ...   "
Low Calorie
    Thousand
    Island .... 25 ...   "

B. MANISCHEWITZ COMPANY

Gefilte Fish
    (Jumbo) ..... 64 ...each
Whitefish &
    Pike .... 40 ...   "

Borscht .... 72 ...8 ozs.
Schav .... 11 ...   "
Lo Cal Borscht .. 24 ...   "
Vegetarian Vege-
    table Soup ... 62 ...   "
Chicken Vege-
    table Soup ... 54 ...   "
Split Pea Soup ..132 ...   "
Bean Soup .....111 ...   "
Tomato Soup .... 60 ...   "
Tomato & Rice
    Soup .... 77 ...   "
Lima Bean
    Soup .... 93 ...   "
Lentil Soup .....166 ...   "
Beef Noodle
    Soup .... 63 ...   "
Beef Barley
    Soup .... 83 ...   "
Beef Cabbage
    Soup .... 61 ...   "
Beef Vegetable
    Soup .... 58 ...   "
Clear Chicken
    Soup .... 45 ...per can

Egg n' Onion
Matzo . . . . 112 . . . each
Regular Matzo . . 121 . . . "
Thin Tea Matzo . . 109 . . . "
Tasteas . . . . 139 . . . "
Matzo Thins . . . . 90 . . . "
Whole Wheat
Matzo . . . . 126 . . . "
Egg Matzo . . . . . 136 . . . "
Tam Tam
Crackers . . . . . 13 . . . "
Onion Tam
Crackers . . . . . 13 . . . "

MINUTE MAID COMPANY
(Minute Maid, Snow Crop, Hi-C, Alegre)
Frozen Products
Orange Juice . . . . 90 . . . 6 ozs.
Grapefruit
Juice . . . . 75 . . . "
Orange-Grapefruit
Blend . . . . 76 . . . "
Tangerine Juice,
Sweetened . . . 85 . . . "
Grape Juice,
Sweetened . . . 99 . . . "
Lemon Juice . . . . 40 . . . "
Lemonade . . . . . 74 . . . "
Limeade . . . . 75 . . . "
Lemon-
Limeade . . . . . 75 . . . "
Orangeade . . . . . 94 . . . "
Bright & Early . . . 100 . . . "
Minute Maid
Chilled Orange
Juice . . . . 83 . . . "

HI-C FRUIT DRINKS
Orange . . . . 98 . . . "
Grape . . . . 98 . . . "
Florida Punch . . . 98 . . . "
Orange-
Pineapple . . . . 98 . . . "
Apple . . . . 90 . . . "
Cherry Red . . . . . 90 . . . "
Wild Berry . . . . . . 90 . . . "
Strawberry
Cooler . . . . 98 . . . "

Citrus Cooler . . . 90 . . . 6 ozs.
Alegre
Mango-
Pineapple . . . . 140 . . . "
Red Tropical
Fruit Punch . . . 98 . . . "
Paradise Peach . . 93 . . . "
Island Orange . . . 102 . . . "

NABISCO (National Biscuit Company)

Bacon Flavored
Thins
Crackers . . . . . 10 . . . each
Butter Flavored
Thins
Crackers . . . . . 15 . . . "
Cheese-Nips
Crackers . . . . . 5 . . . "
Cheese Tid-Bit
Crackers . . . . . 4 . . . "
Chicken in a
Biskit . . . . 10 . . . "
Chippers Potato
Crackers . . . . . 14 . . . "
Chit Chat Barbe-
cue Crackers . . 14 . . . "
Crown Pilot
Crackers . . . . . 73 . . . "
Dandy Soup
and Oyster
Crackers . . . . . 3 . . . "
French Onion
Crackers . . . . . 11 . . . "
Holland Rusk . . . 50 . . . "
Merry Makers
Crackers . . . . . 12 . . . "
Meal Mates
Sesame Bread
Wafers . . . . . . 22 . . . "
Nabisco Graham
Crackers . . . . . 30 . . . "
Nabisco Sugar
Honey
Grahams . . . . . 30 . . . "
Nabisco Sugar
Honey Grahams
(West Coast) . . 30 . . . "

Nabisco
Zwieback .... 31...each

Oysterettes Soup
& Oyster
Crackers ..... 3... "

Premium Crackers
(Unsalted
Tops) .... 14... "

Premium Saltine
Crackers ..... 14... "

Ritz Cheese
Crackers ..... 18... "

Cheese n' Bacon
Flavored
Sandwich ....196...per packet

Cheese-Nips
Crackers .....195... "

Cheese-on-Rye
Crackers ...209... "

Cheese Tid-Bit
Crackers .....192... "

Cheese Peanut
Butter
Sandwich ....230... "

Devil's Food
Cakes ....192... "

Fancy Peanut
Creme
Patties ......192... "

Fig Newtons
Cakes ....269... "

Lorna Doone
Shortbread ...242... "

Malted Milk
Peanut Butter
Sandwich ....224... "

Merri Rolls Creme
Filled Cakes ..110... "

Merri Rolls Creme
Filled Cakes
Mint Flavor ...110... "

Peanut Creme
Patties ......274... "

Nabisco Salted
Peanuts .....267... "

Nabisco Sugar
Wafers ......220... "

Oreo Creme
Sandwich ....239...per packet

O-So-Gud Cheese
Peanut Butter
Sandwich ....145... "

Premium Saltine
Crackers .....114... "

Sociables
Crackers .....202... "

Swiss Creme
Sandwich ....260... "

Triangle Thins ..203... "

Veri-Thin Pretzel
Sticks .... 79... "
Cookie Treats ... 30... "

Dandy Soup &
Oyster
Crackers ..... 75... "

Gem Soup & Chili
Crackers ..... 91... "

Meal Mates
Sesame Bread
Wafers ...... 44... "

Melba Snacks ....16... "

Melba Toast .... 30... "

Premium Saltine
Crackers ..... 28... "

Ritz Crackers ... 35... "

Triscuit Wafers ...43... "

Waverly Wafers .. 36... "

Cracker Meal,
Salted .....308...3 oz.

Cracker Meal,
Unsalted .....318... "

Graham Cracker
Crumbs ......535...1¼ cups

Cream of Wheat
Cereal ....100...1 oz. dry

Nabisco 100%
Bran .... 75...½ cup

Nabisco Rice
Honeys
Cereal ....113...¾ cup

Nabisco Shredded
Wheat
Biscuits ..... 94...each

Spoon Size
Shredded
Wheat .... 7... "

Home Style
Cinnamon
Sugar
Cookies ...... 48...each
Home Style
Cinnamon
Rings
Cookies ...... 47... "
Home Style Fudge
Rings
Cookies ...... 45... "
Hoo-Ray Toasted
Cocoanut
Caramel
Logs ....102... "
Ideal Chocolate
Peanut Bars .. 94... "
Jonnie Cakes ... 56... "
Kettle Cookies ... 30... "
Lemon Snaps ... 16... "
Lorna Doone
Shortbread ... 38... "
Mallomars Choco-
late Cakes .... 59... "
Marshmallow
Sandwich .... 32... "
Melody Chocolate
Cookies .... 31... "
Merri Rolls Creme
Filled ......119... "
Minaret Cakes ... 46... "
Nabisco Chocolate
Fudge
Sandwich .... 53... "
Nabisco Chocolate
Marshmallow
Eclairs ...... 86... "
Nabisco Chocolate
Pinwheels ....139... "
Nabisco Date &
Nut Cookies .. 78... "
Nabisco Devil's
Food Cakes ... 57... "
Nabisco Fancy
Crests Cakes .. 70... "
Nabisco Fancy
Grahams ..... 68... "
Nabisco Iced Fruit
Cookies ...... 70... "

Nabisco Macaroon
Sandwich .... 71...each
Nabisco
Marshmallow
Twirls ....133...each
Nabisco Peanut
Creme
Patties ...... 34... "
Nabisco Pecan
Shortbread
Cookies .... 77... "
Nabisco Raisin
Fruit Biscuit .. 56... "
Nabisco Spiced
Wafers ...... 33... "
Nabisco Striped
Shortbread ... 50... "
Nabisco Sugar
Wafers ...... 18... "
Nabisco Vanilla
Wafers ...... 18... "
National Arrowroot
Biscuits ..... 22... "
Old-Fashion
Ginger
Snaps .... 30... "
Oreo Creme
Sandwich .... 50... "
Robena
Grahams ..... 71... "
Social Tea
Biscuit ...... 21... "
Swiss Rolls Creme
Filled ......119... "
Waffle Cremes .. 55... "
Zu Zu Ginger
Snaps .... 16... "

Bake Shop
Chocolate Chip
Pastry ....235...per packet
Bake Shop Coffee
Crunch
Wafers ......227... "
Bake Shop
Cocoanut
Honey Pastry ..230... "
Bake Shop Date
Nut Pastry .. 200... "

95

Bake Shop
  Nut Fudge
  Brownies ....265...per packet
Bake Shop Peanut
  Crunch
  Wafers ......221...   "
Ritz Crackers ... 18...each
Sky Flake
  Wafers ...... 15...   "
Snow Flake
  Crackers ..... 14...   "
Snow Flake
  Saltine
  Crackers ..... 14...   "
Sociables
  Crackers ..... 10...   "
Swiss n' Ham
  Flavored
  Crackers ..... 11...   "
Tang-O Chips ... 9...   "
Triangle Thins
  Crackers ..... 8...   "
Triscuit Wafers .. 22...   "
Uneeda Biscuit
  (Unsalted
  Tops) .... 22...   "
Warm Welcome
  Crackers ..... 13...   "
Waverly Wafers .. 18...   "
Wheat Thins
  Crackers ..... 9...   "
Dutch Pretzels .. 51...   "
Pretzelettes .... 6...   "
3-Ring Pretzels .. 12...   "
Veri-Thin
  Pretzels ..... 20...   "
Veri-Thin Pretzels
  Sticks .... 1...   "
Bake Shop
  Cocoanut
  Macaroons ... 87...   "
Barnum's Animal
  Crackers ..... 12...   "
Baronet Creme
  Sandwich .... 55...   "
Brown Edge
  Wafers ...... 28...   "
Brownie Bars ... 55...   "

Brownie Thin
  Wafers ...... 40...each
Brownie Thin
  Wafers,
  Vanilla ...... 36...   "
Butter Flavored
  Cookies ...... 37...   "
Cameo Creme
  Sandwich .... 68...   "
Cameo Fudge
  Filled
  Sandwich .... 69...each
Cashew Nut
  Cookies ...... 57...   "
Chiparoons Cocoa-
  nut Chocolate
  Drop Cookies .. 76...   "
Chipits Chocolate
  Chip Pecan
  Cookies ...... 55...   "
Chocolate Almond
  Cookies ...... 55...   "
Chocolate Chip
  Cookies ...... 51...   "
Chocolate Chip
  Snaps .... 21...   "
Chocolate
  Grahams ..... 55...   "
Chocolate
  Snaps .... 18...   "
Cinnamon Almond
  Cookies ...... 53...   "
Cookie Treats
  Fig Cakes .... 58...   "
Cowboys and
  Indians
  Cookies ...... 9...   "
Dairy Wafers
  Round ...... 49...   "
Family Favorites
  Brown Sugar
  Cookies ...... 25...   "
Family Favorites
  Chocolate Chip
  Cookies ...... 33...   "
Family Favorites
  Cocoanut
  Cookies ...... 16...   "

Family Favorite
  Hermit
  Cookies . . . . . . 25 . . . each
Famous Chocolate
  Wafers . . . . . . 28 . . . "
Fig Newtons
  Cakes . . . . 56 . . . "
Home Style
  Cashew
  Shortbread
  Cookies . . . . . . 49 . . . "
Home Style
  Chocolate Chip
  Cookies . . . . . . 51 . . . "
Wheat Honeys
  Cereal . . . . . . 114 . . . ¾ cup

NESTLÉ COMPANY

Maggi Instant
  Bouillon,
  Beef . . . . 8 . . . 1 cube
Maggi Instant
  Bouillon,
  Chicken . . . . . 8 . . .   "
Quik Chocolate . . 80 . . . 2 heaping
                              tsp.
Quik
  Strawberry . . . 80 . . .   "
Semi-Sweet
  Chocolate
  Morsels . . . . . 150 . . . 1 oz.
Semi-Sweet Mint
  Chocolate
  Morsels . . . . . 150 . . . "
Milk Chocolate
  Morsels . . . . . 150 . . . "
Butterscotch
  Morsels . . . . . 150 . . . "
Milk Chocolate
  Bars:
  Plain . . . . 150 . . . "
  Crunch . . . . . . 140 . . . "
  Almond . . . . . . 150 . . . "
  Choco'Lite . . . 140 . . . "
  $100,000 . . . . 130 . . . "
Nescafe Instant
  Coffee . . . . 4 . . . 1 tsp.

Decaf Instant
  Coffee . . . . 4 . . . 1 tsp.
Taster's Choice
  Instant
  Coffee . . . . 4 . . . "
Taster's Choice
  Decaffeinated
  Instant
  Coffee . . . . 4 . . . "

Instant Nestea
  (100% tea) . . . 0 . . . "
Lemon Nestea . . 2 . . . "
Nestea Iced Tea
  Mix . . . . 60 . . . 1 tbsp.
Hot Cocoa Mix . . 25 . . . 1 heaping
                              tsp.

OSCAR MAYER

Fresh Pork Sausage
Fresh Sausage,
  cooked . . . . . 50 . . . 1 oz.
Pork Sausage
  Links (14-18
  per lb.) . . . . . . 50 . . . per link
Links
Beef Franks
  (10 per lb.) . . . 145 . . . per link
Breakfast Sausage
  Links (7 per
  5 oz.) . . . . 70 . . . "
Brotwurst (4 per
  ¾ lb.) . . . . 280 . . . "
Cheese Smokies
  (8 per ¾ lb.) . . 135 . . . "
Chubbies Sausage
  (5 per ¾ lb.) . . 210 . . . "
1883 Brand
  Franks
  (6 per lb.) . . . . 215 . . . "
Imperial Wieners
  (5 per lb.) . . . . 280 . . . "
Kielbasa
  (12 oz.) . . . . . . 90 . . . 1 oz.
Little Smokies
  (16 per 5 oz.) . . 30 . . . per link

Little Wieners
(16 per 5½
oz.) . . . . 30. . .per link
Machiaeh Franks
(8 per lb.) . . . .180. . .   "
Polish Sausage
(2 per lb.) . . . . 95. . .1 oz.
Ring Bologna
(¾ lb.) . . . . . . 90. . .1 oz.
Smokie Links
(8 per ¾ lb.) . .135. . .per link
Wieners
(10 per lb.) . . .145. . .per link

Meat Spreads
Braunschweiger
Liver
Sausage . . . . .100. . .1 oz.
Ham & Cheese
Spread . . . . . . 75. . .2 tbsps.
Ham Salad
Spread . . . . . . 60. . .   "
Sandwich
Spread . . . . . . 65. . .   "
Smoky Snax
Spread . . . . . .100. . .   "

Sliced Cold Meats
Beef Bologna
(10 slices
per ½ lb.) . . . . 70. . .per slice
Beef Cotto
Salami (10
slices per
½ lb.) . . . . 50. . .   "
Beef Luncheon
Meat . . . . 80. . .per oz.
Beef Summer
Sausage
(10 slices
per ½ lb.) . . . . 65. . .per slice
Bologna . . . . 90. . .per oz.
Cotto Salami
(10 slices
per ½ lb.) . . . . 55. . .per slice
German Brand
Bologna
(10 slices
per ½ lb.) . . . . 55. . .   "

Hard Salami . . . .110. . .per oz.
Honey Loaf . . . . . 40. . .   "
Jellied Corned
Beef Loaf . . . . 40. . .   "
Lebanon Bologna
(10 slices
per ½ lb.) . . . . 45. . .per slice
Liver Cheese
(6 slices
per ½ lb.) . . . .100. . .   "
Luncheon Meat . . 95. . .per oz.
Luncheon Roll
Sausage
(10 slices
per ½ lb.) . . . . 30. . .per slice
Luxury Loaf . . . . . 40. . .per oz.
Machiaeh Salami
(10 slices
per ½ lb.) . . . . 60. . .per slice
New England
Brand
Sausage
(10 slices
per ½ lb.) . . . . 35. . .   "
Old Fashioned
Loaf . . . . 60. . .per oz.
Olive Loaf . . . . . . 60. . .   "
Peppered Loaf . . 45. . .   "
Pickle & Pimiento
Loaf (cocktail
loaf) . . . . 65. . .   "
Picnic Loaf . . . . . 60. . .   "
Salami For Beer
(10 slices
per ½ lb.) . . . . 50. . .per slice

Smoked Meats
Bacon (regular,
18-26 slices
per lb.) . . . . . . 40. . .per cooked
                                slice
Bacon (thick,
11-14 slices
per lb.) . . . . . . 65. . .   "
Bacon (thin,
25-30 slices
per ¾ lb.) . . . . 25. . .   "
Canadian Style
Bacon . . . . 40. . .1 oz.

Canned hams
(oblong/
pear) .... 35...1 oz.
Chopped Ham ... 65...1 oz.
Cooked Ham
(8 slices
per 6 oz.) .... 30...per slice
Ham slice ...... 40...1 oz.
Ham Steak
(2 oz.) .... 70...per steak
Minced Ham
(10 slices
per ½ lb.) .... 55...per slice
Smoked Hams,
boneless ..... 50...1 oz.
Sweet Morsel
(pork shoulder),
cooked ...... 65...1 oz.

RALSTON PURINA COMPANY

Ralston Oats,
Quick and
Regular ......104...5 tbsp. dry
Ralston Cereal,
Regular ......110...4 tbsp. dry
Ralston Instant
Cereal ......110...4 tbsp. dry
Corn Chex ......110...1¼ cups
Ralston Corn
Flakes ....110...1 cup
Rice Chex ......110...1⅛ cups
Wheat Chex .....110...⅔ cup
Ry-Krisp .... 25...each cracker
Ry-Krisp,
Seasoned .... 30...each cracker

S & W NUTRADIET FOODS
(Dietetic Pack)
Blue Label
(unsweetened and unseasoned)
Applesauce ..... 48...½ cup
Apricots,
Halves ...... 38...4 halves
Cherries, Royal
Anne .... 47...14 whole
Figs, Whole ..... 52... 6   "
Fruit Cocktail ... 35...½ cup

Peaches, Cling
Slices .... 24...½ cup
Peaches, Cling
Halves ...... 28...2 halves
Pears, Halves ... 30...   "
Pears,
Quartered .... 27...½ cup
Pineapple,
Sliced .... 69...2½ slices
Pineapple
Tidbits ...... 69...½ cup
Salad Fruits .... 38...   "

Asparagus, All
Green .... 16...5 whole
Beans, Cut
Green .... 16...½ cup
Beets, Sliced .... 28...   "
Carrots, Sliced .. 22...   "
Corn, Cream
Style .... 84...   "
Corn, Whole
Kernel ...... 52...   "
Peas, Sweet .... 35...   "
Peas & Carrots .. 32...
Tomatoes,
Whole .... 21...   "
Apricot & Pine-
apple Nectar .. 31...   "
Grape Juice .... 60...   "
Pineapple
Juice ...... 59...   "
Tomato Juice ... 22...   "
Vegetable Juice
Cocktail ..... 21...   "

Salmon .... 84...¼ tin

Red Label (with calorie-free sweetener)
Applesauce ..... 48...½ cup
Apricot, Halves .. 40...4 halves
Apricots,
Whole .... 31...2 whole
Blackberries .... 36...½ cup
Boysenberries ... 32...   "
Cherries, Royal
Anne .... 49...14 whole

Cherries, Dark
Sweet .... 53...½ cup
Figs, Whole ..... 49...6 whole
Fruit Cocktail ... 36...½ cup
Grapefruit
Sections ..... 35... "
Peaches, Cling
Halves ...... 25...2 halves
Peaches, Cling
Slices .... 25...½ cup
Peaches, Free-
stone Halves .. 26...2 halves
Peaches, Free-
stone Slices .. 24...½ cup
Pears, Halves ... 28...2 halves
Pears,
Quartered .....26...½ cup
Pineapple,
Chunks ...... 49... "
Pineapple,
Sliced .... 56...2½ slices
Pineapple,
Tidbits ...... 49...½ cup
Purple Plums ... 50... "
Salad Fruits .... 35... "
Strawberries .... 20... "

Apricot Nectar .. 31... "
Pear Nectar .... 30... "

Apple Jelly ..... 1.4...1 tsp.
Apricot-Pineapple
Preserves .... 1.6... "
Blackberry Jam .. 1.7... "
Red Tart
Cherry
Preserves .... 1.9... "
Concord Grape
Jelly .... 1.9... "
Raspberry Jam .. 1.5... "
Strawberry
Jam .... 1.4... "
S & W
Imitation Maple
Syrup .... 4...1 tsp.
All Purpose
Nutradiet
Sweetener ... 0... "

SEABROOK FARMS CO.

Frozen Barbecue
Beef .... 41...1 oz.
Frozen Beef
Goulash with
Noodles ..... 28... "
Frozen Beef in
Red Wine
Sauce .... 44... "
Frozen Beef
Stew .... 29... "
Frozen Breast of
Chicken
Cacciatore ... 35... "
Frozen Chicken
Leg with
Gravy .... 44... "
Frozen Ham in
Raisin Sauce .. 44... "
Frozen Macaroni
and Beef ..... 31... "
Frozen Macaroni
and Cheese .. 31... "
Frozen Meat Balls
in Tomato
Sauce .... 36... "
Frozen Sliced
Beef with
Gravy .... 35... "
Frozen Sliced
Turkey with
Gravy .... 31... "
Frozen Swiss
Steak .... 49...1 oz.

Frozen Asparagus
Cuts and
Tips .... 21... "
Frozen Creamed
Spinach ..... 26... "
Frozen French
Fried Onion
Rings .... 42... "
Frozen Green
Beans with
Mushroom
Sauce .... 25... "

Frozen Lima Beans
in Cheese
Sauce . . . . 35 . . . 1 oz.
Frozen Peas in
Onion Sauce . . 24 . . .   "

SEALTEST FOODS
(National Dairy Products Corp.)

Whole Milk, Vit.
D added . . . . . 151 . . .8 oz.
Chocolate
Drink . . . . . . .154 . . .   "
Chocolate Milk . .205 . . .   "
Skim Milk . . . . . . 81 . . .   "
Diet Skim Milk . .105 . . .   "
Vita Lure . . . . . . .137 . . .   "
n-r-g® . . . . .127 . . .   "
Multivitamin
Milk . . . . .151 . . .   "
Cultured
Buttermilk . . .100 . . .   "
Yogurt, Plain . . . .144 . . .   "
Sweetened Con-
densed Milk . . 64 . . .1 tbsp.
Evaporated
Milk . . . . .173 . . .4 oz.
Dried Whole
Milk . . . . .141 . . .4 tbsps.
Nonfat Dry Milk
Solids . . . . . . .102 . . .   "
Plain Malted
Milk . . . . .118 . . .3 tbsps.
Chocolate Malted
Milk . . . . .115 . . .   "

Cream . . . . 26 . . .1 tbsp.
Light, Table or
Coffee
Cream . . . . . . 28 . . .   "
Whipping
Cream . . . . . . 44 . . .1 tbsp.
Heavy Cream . . . 52 . . .   "
Cultured or
Sour Cream . . 57 . . .2 tbsps.
Half and Half . . .150 . . .4 oz.

Butter . . . . 73 . . .2 tsps.

Creamed Cottage
Cheese . . . . . . 71 . . .⅓ cup
Uncreamed Cot-
tage Cheese . . 60 . . .   "
Spring Garden
Salad Creamed
Cottage
Cheese . . . . . . 70 . . .   "
Pineapple
Creamed
Cottage
Cheese . . . . . . 67 . . .   "

Dip 'n' Dressing,
French
Onion . . . . 92 . . .2 oz.

Vanilla Ice
Cream . . . . . .176 . . .⅙ qt.
Chocolate Ice
Cream . . . . . .191 . . .   "
Strawberry Ice
Cream . . . . . .174 . . .   "
Vanilla Fudge
Royale Ice
Cream . . . . . .183 . . .   "
Prestige French
Vanilla Ice
Cream . . . . . .247 . . .   "

Prestige French
Chocolate Ice
Cream . . . . . .250 . . .   "
Vanilla Ice Cream
Slice . . . . .133 . . .⅛ qt.
Ice Cream Bar
Chocolate
Flavor
Coating . . . . .162 . . .3 fl. oz.
Ice Cream
Sandwich . . . .208 . . .1 sandwich
Vanilla Ice Milk . .135 . . .⅙ qt.
Ice Milk Bar Choc-
olate Flavor
Coating . . . . .144 . . .3 fl. oz.
Orange Sherbet . .152 . . .⅙ qt.
Orange Ice . . . . .177 . . .   "
3 oz. Popsicle . . . 95 . . .4 fl. oz.

American Process
   Cheese . . . . . . 105 . . . 1 oz.
American Cheddar
   Cheese . . . . . . 154 . . .   ″
Domestic Swiss
   Cheese . . . . . . 105 . . .   ″
Cheese Spread,
   Pimiento . . . . 77 . . .   ″
Cream Cheese . . 98 . . .   ″

Orange Juice . . . . 64 . . . 4 oz.
Deluxe Orange
   Drink . . . . . . 111 . . . 8 oz.
Deluxe Grapefruit
   Drink . . . . . . 107 . . .   ″
Lemonade . . . . . 104 . . .   ″
Grape Ade . . . . . 126 . . .   ″
Orange Ade . . . . . 124 . . .   ″

Oleomargarine . . 73 . . . 2 tsps.
Frozen Dessert . . 180 . . . ⅙ qt.
Eggnog . . . . 177 . . . 4 oz.

SEGO (Pet Milk Co.)

Sego Liquid Diet
   Foods, all
   flavors . . . . . . 225 . . . per can

SEVEN SEAS SALAD DRESSINGS (Anderson, Clayton & Co. Foods Division)

Coach House
   Salad
   Dressing . . . . . 26 . . . per tsp.
Regular Italian
   Salad
   Dressing . . . . . 27 . . .   ″
Creamy Italian
   Salad
   Dressing . . . . . 27 . . .   ″
Creamy Russian
   Salad
   Dressing . . . . . 24 . . .   ″
Creamy French
   Salad
   Dressing . . . . . 21 . . .   ″

Sweet Dutch
   Salad
   Dressing . . . . . 20 . . . per tsp.
Low Calorie
   French
   Dressing . . . . . 5 . . .   ″
Low Calorie Italian
   Dressing . . . . . 5 . . . per tsp.
Green Goddess
   Salad
   Dressing . . . . . 26 . . .   ″

THE J.M. SMUCKER COMPANY

Slenderella Low Sugar Jams and Jellies
Imitation Apple
   Jelly . . . . 8 . . . 1 tsp.
Imitation Apricot
   Jam . . . . 9 . . .   ″
Imitation
   Blackberry
   Jelly . . . . 8 . . .   ″
Imitation
   Blackberry
   Apple Jelly . . . 8 . . .   ″
Imitation
   Boysenberry
   Jelly . . . . 8 . . .   ″
Imitation
   Cherry Jelly . . 9 . . .   ″
Imitation
   Grape Jelly . . . 8 . . .   ″
Imitation Orange
   Marmalade . . . 8 . . .   ″
Imitation
   Strawberry
   Jam . . . . 8 . . .   ″

Smucker's Artificially Sweetened Jams and Jellies
Imitation Grape
   Jelly . . . . 1 . . . 1 tsp.
Imitation
   Strawberry
   Jam . . . . 1 . . .   ″

Fruit Butters, Preserves, and Jellies

Peach Butter .... 30...2 tsps.
Spiced and Cider
   Apple Butter .. 25...   "
Orange
   Marmalade ... 35...   "
Smucker
   Preserves .... 35...   "
Smucker
   Jellies .... 35...   "
Goober Grape ...250...2 ozs.
Goober
   Strawberry ...250...   "
Goober
   Raspberry ....250...   "
Creamy Peanut
   Butter ....180...1 oz.
Crunchy Peanut
   Butter ....180...   "
Pure Peanut
   Butter ....190...   "
Butterscotch
   Topping ..... 70...1 tbsp.
Caramel
   Topping ..... 70...   "
Chocolate Flavor
   Syrup
   Topping ..... 65...   "
Chocolate Fudge
   Topping ..... 65...   "
Chocolate Mint
   Fudge
   Topping ..... 70...   "
Cherry Topping .. 65...   "
Peanut Butter
   Caramel
   Topping ..... 75...   "
Pecans in Syrup
   Topping ..... 75...   "
Pineapple
   Topping ..... 65...   "
Strawberry
   Topping ..... 60...   "
Swiss Milk
   Chocolate
   Topping ..... 70...   "
Walnuts in Syrup
   Topping ..... 75...   "

STANDARD BRANDS PRODUCTS

Royal Pudding (Regular)

Chocolate ......190...½ cup
Vanilla ....160...   "
Butterscotch ....190...   "
Dark 'N' Sweet ..190...   "
Banana ....160...   "
Chocolate
   Tapioca .....190...   "
Vanilla
   Tapioca .....170...   "
Custard Flavor
   Dessert ......130...   "
Lemon Pie
   Filling ....220...⅛ of 9" pie
                  with
                  meringue
Key Lime Pie
   Filling ......220...   "

Royal Pudding (Instant)

Dark 'N' Sweet ..180...½ cup
Chocolate ......190...½ cup
Vanilla ....170...   "
Butterscotch ....170...   "
Toasted
   Coconut .....180...   "
Banana Cream ..170...   "
Lemon ....180...   "
Caramel Nut ....190...   "
Mocha Nut .....200...   "
Pistachio Nut ...180...   "
Royal Gelatin
   Desserts ..... 80...   "

Royal No Bake
   Cheese Cake ..280...⅛ of 9" pie

Chase & Sanborn
   Coffee,
   regular ...... 1...1 cup
Chase & Sanborn
   Instant
   Coffee ...... 1...   "
Tender Leaf Tea
   Bags .... 1...1 cup

Tender Leaf
Instant Tea . . .   1 . . . 1 cup
Tender Leaf
Iced Tea Mix . . 60 . . . 1 glass
Tender Leaf Lo-Cal
Lemon Tea
Mix . . . . 10 . . .   "

Fleischmann's
Active Dry
Yeast . . . . 20 . . . ¼ oz.
Fresh Active,
Yeast Cake . . . 20 . . . ⅜ oz.

Salted
Margarine . . . . 50 . . . 1 pat
Unsalted
Margarine . . . . 50 . . .   "
Soft Margarine . . 50 . . .   "
Egg Beaters . . . . 90 . . . ¼ cup
Corn Oil . . . . 120 . . . 1 tbsp.

Royal Baking
Powder . . . . . .   5 . . . 1 tsp.

Planters
Peanut Butter . . . 190 . . . 2 tbsp.
Jumbo Peanut
Block Candy
Bar . . . . 140 . . . 1 oz.
Cashew Crunch
Candy Bar . . . . 135 . . .   "
Oil Roasted Pea-
nuts, Can . . . . 170 . . .   "
Oil Roasted Cash-
ews, Can . . . . . 170 . . .   "
Oil Roasted Mixed
Nuts (with Pea-
nuts), Can . . . . 180 . . .   "
Oil Roasted Mixed
Nuts (without
Peanuts)
Can . . . . 180 . . .   "
Spanish Peanuts,
Can . . . . 170 . . .   "
Dry Roasted Pea-
nuts, Jar . . . . . 160 . . .   "
Dry Roasted Cash-
ews, Jar . . . . . 160 . . .   "

Dry Roasted Mixed
Nuts, Jar . . . . . 170 . . . 1 oz.
Dry Roasted Span-
ish Peanuts . . . 160 . . .   "
Dry Roasted
Pecans . . . . . . 190 . . .   "
Dry Roasted
Almonds . . . . . 180 . . .   "
Peanut Oil,
Bottle . . . . 120 . . . 1 tbsp.

Blue Bonnet Margarine
Regular . . . . 50 . . . 1 pat
Whipped . . . . 30 . . .   "
Soft . . . . 50 . . .   "

STAR-KIST FOODS, INC.

Packed in Vegetable Oil (Includes Oil)
Solid Style
Canned White
Tuna . . . . 520 . . . 7 oz. can
Solid Style
Canned White
Tuna . . . . 740 . . . 10 oz. can
Chunk Style
Canned Light
Tuna . . . . 460 . . . 6½ oz. can
Chunk Style
Canned Light
Tuna . . . . 230 . . . 3¼ oz. can
Chunk Style
Canned Light
Tuna . . . . 650 . . . 9¼ oz. can
Chunk Style
Canned White
Tuna . . . . 690 . . .   "

Packed in Spring Water
Solid Style
Canned White
Tuna . . . . 240 . . . 7 oz. can
Solid Style
Canned White
Tuna . . . . 340 . . . 10 oz. can
Solid Style
Canned Light
Tuna . . . . 230 . . . 7 oz. can

Packed in Distilled Water

Diet Pack Canned
  Chunk White
  Tuna . . . . .240. . .6½ oz. can
Diet Pack Canned
  Chunk White
  Tuna . . . . .120. . .3¼ oz. can

Star-Kist Frozen
  Tuna Pies . . . .450. . .8 ozs.

STOKELY-VAN CAMP, INC.

Van Camp's Brown
  Sugar Beans . .390. . .1 cup
Van Camp's Pork
  and Beans . . .260. . .1 cup

SUNSHINE BISCUITS, INC.

Animal Cookies . . 10. . .each
Applesauce
  Cookies . . . . . 86. . . "
Arrowroot
  Cookies . . . . . 16. . . "
Butter Flavored
  Cookies . . . . .153. . . "
Cheez-Its . . . . . . 6. . . "
Chip-A-Roos
  (large) . . . . . . 63. . . "
Chocolate Chip
  Coconut
  Cookies . . . . . 80. . . "
Chocolate Fudge
  Cookies . . . . . 72. . . "
Cinnamon Toast
  Cookies . . . . . 13. . . "
Coconut Bar
  Cookies . . . . . 47. . . "
Crackermeal . . . .400. . .100 grams.
Cup Custard,
  Chocolate . . . . 70. . .each
Cup Custard,
  Vanilla . . . . . . 71. . . "
Dixie Vanilla . . . . 60. . . "
Fig Bars . . . . 45. . . "
Ginger Snaps . . . 24. . . "
Golden Fruit . . . . 61. . . "
Graham
  Crumbs . . . . .420. . .100 grams.

HiHo Cookies . . . 18. . .each
Hydrox Cookies . . 48. . . "
Hydrox, Vanilla
  Cookies . . . . . 50. . . "
Iced Animal
  Cookies . . . . . 26. . . "
Iced Applesauce
  Cookies . . . . . 86. . . "
Iced Oatmeal
  Cookies . . . . . 69. . . "
Krispy Crackers. . 11. . .each
Krispy Crackers
  (RS) . . . . 12. . . "
Lady Joan Cookies
  (Iced) . . . . 42. . . "
Lady Joan
  (Plain) . . . . . . 47. . . "
LaLanne
  Sesame . . . . . 15. . . "
LaLanne Soya . . . 16. . . "
Lemon Cookies . . 76. . . "
Lemon Coolers . . 29. . . "
Mallopuffs . . . . . 63. . . "
Molasses &
  Spice . . . . 67. . . "
Oatmeal
  Cookies . . . . . 58. . . "
Oatmeal Peanut
  Butter
  Cookies . . . . . 79. . . "
Orbit Creme
  Sandwich . . . . 51. . . "
Oysters, Mini
  Crackers . . . . . 3. . . "

Peanut Butter
  Patties . . . . . . 33. . . "
Scotties . . . . 39. . . "
Soda Crackers . . 20. . . "
Sprinkles . . . . . . 57. . . "
Sugar Wafers . . . 43. . . "
Sugar Wafers
  (Lemon) . . . . . 44. . . "
Toy Cookies . . . . 13. . . "
Vanilla Wafers,
  Small . . . . 15. . . "
Vienna Finger
  Sandwich . . . . 71. . . "

Yum Yums . . . . . 83. . . "

SUNSWEET GROWERS INC.

Prune, Medium . . 13 . . .each
Prune, Large . . . . 17 . . . "
Prune, Extra
    Large . . . . . . 20 . . . "
Pitted Prune . . . . 19 . . . "
Prune Juice . . . . 20 . . .1 oz.

THE UNDERWOOD COMPANY
(Underwood, R & R)

Underwood
Deviled Ham . . . .226 . . .2¼ oz. can
Deviled Ham . . . .453 . . .4½ oz. can
Liver Spread . . . .428 . . .4¾ oz. can
Chicken Spread . .309 . . .   "
Sardines—
   Oil, Red
   Devil . . . . . . .209 . . .3¾ oz. can
   Mustard, Red
     Devil . . . . .168 . . .   "
   Tomato, Red
     Devil . . . . .155 . . .   "
   Mooseabec . . .225 . . .4 oz. can

R & R
Boned Chicken . .328 . . .5½ oz. can
Chicken Broth,
   clear . . . . 21 . . .12½ oz.
Chicken Broth
   w/Rice . . . . . . 59 . . .   "

Chicken
   Fricassee . . . .343 . . .14 oz.
Chicken A La
   King . . . . .332 . . .10½ oz.

VAN CAMP SEAFOOD COMPANY

Tuna, Solids and
   Liquid . . . . .247 . . .3 oz.
Tuna, Drained
   Solids . . . . . . .169 . . . "

WHITE HOUSE FOOD PRODUCTS

Apple Butter . . . .211 . . .4 oz.
Apple Juice . . . . . 56 . . . "
Apple Sauce,
   sweetened . . .103 . . . "
Apple Sauce, un-
   sweetened . . . 50 . . . "
Apple Cider
   Vinegar . . . . . . 17 . . . "
Spiced Apple
   Rings . . . . 19 . . .per ring
Escalloped
   Apples . . . . . .116 . . .4 oz.

WILSON & COMPANY, INC.

Wilson's Certified Provisions
Fully Cooked
   Canned Ham . . 48 . . .1 oz.

Smoked Festival		
Ham	48...	**1 oz.**
Bacon, raw	169...	"
Smoked Picnic ..	70...	"
Smoked Tasty		
Meat	72...	"
Canadian		
Bacon	42...	"
Boned & Rolled		
Ham	56...	"

Sausage		
Braun-		
schweiger	89...	"
Bologna	87...	"
Skinless All Meat		
Frankfurter ...	87...	"
All Beef Frank-		
furters	85...	"
Pure Pork		
Sausage	135...	"
Smokies	84...	"
Canned Meats		
Bif	91...	"
Mor	89...	"
Vienna		
Sausage	85...	"
Tender Made		
Ham	44...	"
Tender Made		
Corned Beef		
Brisket	45...	"
Tender Made Pork		
Roast	44...	"
Tender Made		
Turkey Roast ..	29...	"
Tender Made Beef		
Roast	33...	"

Grocery Products		
Chili Con		
Carne	54...	1 oz.
Chili Con Carne		
with Beans ...	41...	"
Corned Beef		
Hash	51...	"
Beef Stew	22...	"
Tamales	39...	"
B V	43...	"

GENERAL CALORIE COUNTS

DAIRY PRODUCTS

Cheeses:
American,
Cheddar type	115	1 oz.
	70	1" cube
	225	½ cup, grated

Process American,
Cheddar type	105	1 oz.
Blue-mold (Roquefort)	105	"
Cottage, not creamed	25	2 tbsps.
Cottage, creamed	30	"
Cream Cheese	105	"
Parmesan, dry, grated	40	"
Swiss	105	1 oz.

Fluid Milk:
Whole	165	1 cup
Skim	90	"
Buttermilk	90	"
Evaporated (undiluted)	170	½ cup
Condensed, sweetened (undiluted)	490	"
Half-and-half (milk and cream)	330	1 cup
	20	1 tbsp.

Milk Beverages:
Cocoa (all milk)	235	1 cup
Chocolate-flavored Milk Drink	190	"
Chocolate Milk Shake	520	12 oz.
Malted Milk	280	1 cup

Others:
Butter	100	1 tbsp.
Cream, light	35	"
Cream, heavy whipping	55	"
Ice Cream, plain	130	3½ oz.
Ice Cream Soda, chocolate	455	1 glass
Ice Milk	140	½ cup
Yoghurt (partially skimmed milk)	120	1 cup

MEATS & POULTRY
(Cooked, without bone)

Beef:
Pot Roast or Braised		
Lean and fat	245	3 oz.
Lean only	140	2½ oz.
Oven Roast		
Lean and fat	220	3 oz.
Lean only	130	2½ oz.
Steak, broiled		
Lean and fat	330	3 oz.
Lean only	115	2 oz.
Hamburger		
Regular ground beef	245	3 oz. patty
Lean ground round	185	"
Corned Beef, canned	180	3 oz.
Corned Beef Hash, canned	120	"
Dried Beef, chipped	115	2 oz.
Meat Loaf	115	"
Beef and Vegetable Stew	90	½ cup
Beef Potpie, baked	460	1 pie, 4¼" dia.

Veal:
Cutlet, broiled (meat only)	185	3 oz.

Chicken:
Broiled	185	3 oz.
Fried	215	½ breast
	245	Thigh and drumstick
Canned	190	½ cup

Lamb:
Chop		
Lean and fat	405	4 oz.
Lean only	140	2-3/5 oz.
Roast Leg		
Lean and fat	235	3 oz.
Lean only	130	2½ oz.

Pork:
Chop		
Lean and fat	260	2⅓ oz.
Lean only	130	2 oz.
Roast Loin		
Lean and fat	310	3 oz.
Lean only	175	2-2/5 oz.
Ham, Cured		
Lean and fat	290	3 oz.
Lean only	125	2-1/5 oz.
Bacon, broiled	95	2 thin slices

Sausage & Variety Meats:
Bologna Sausage	170	2 oz.
Liver Sausage	175	"
Vienna Sausage, canned	135	"
Pork Sausage, bulk	170	2 oz. patty

Beef Liver, fried	120	2 oz.
Beef Tongue, boiled	205	3 oz.
Frankfurter	155	Each
Boiled Ham	170	2 oz.
Spiced Ham, canned	165	"

FISH & SHELLFISH

Bluefish, baked	135	3 oz.
Clams, shelled		
Raw, meat only	70	"
Canned, clams & juice	45	"
Crab Meat	90	"
Fish Sticks	200	4 oz.
Haddock, fried	135	3 oz.
Mackerel		
Broiled	200	"
Canned	155	"
Ocean Perch, fried	195	"
Oysters, raw	80	6 to 10
Salmon		
Broiled	205	4 oz.
Canned (pink)	120	3 oz.
Sardines, canned in oil	180	"
Shrimp, canned	110	"
Tuna, canned in oil	170	"

EGGS

Fried	100	1 large
Boiled	80	"
Scrambled or Omelet	110	"
Poached	80	"

NUTS

Almonds, shelled	105	15 nuts
Brazil Nuts, broken	115	2 tbsps.
Cashew Nuts, roasted	95	5 nuts
Coconut, shredded	40	2 tbsps.
Peanuts, roasted, shelled	105	"
Peanut Butter	90	1 tbsp.
Pecans, shelled	90	12 halves
Walnuts, shelled		
Black	100	2 tbsps.
English	80	10 halves

VEGETABLES

Asparagus	20	6 spears
Beans, fresh		
Lima	75	½ cup
Snap, Green or Wax	15	"
Beans, dried		
Red Kidney, cooked	115	"
Lima, cooked	130	"
Baked		
With pork	165	"
Without pork	160	"
Beets	35	"
Beet Greens, cooked	20	"
Broccoli	20	"
Brussels Sprouts	30	"
Cabbage		
Raw	10	"
Coleslaw (with dressing)	50	"
Cooked	20	"
Carrots	20	"
Cauliflower	15	"
Celery	10	2 large stalks
Chard	25	½ cup
Collards	40	"
Corn on cob	65	1 ear
Corn, cooked	85	½ cup
Cress, Garden	35	"
Cucumbers	5	6 slices
Kale	20	½ cup
Kohlrabi	25	"
Lettuce	5	3 leaves
Mushrooms, canned	15	½ cup
Mustard Greens	15	"
Okra, cooked	15	4 pods
Onions		
Raw	50	1 medium size
Cooked	40	½ cup
Parsnips, cooked	50	"
Peas, Green	60	"
Peppers, Green	15	1 medium
Potatoes		
Baked or boiled	90	"
Chips	110	10 medium
French Fried	155	10 pieces
Hash-browned	235	½ cup
Mashed with milk	70	"
Pan fried	240	"
Radishes	10	4 small
Sauerkraut, canned	15	½ cup
Spinach	20	"
Squash		
Summer	20	"
Winter, baked	50	"
Sweet Potatoes		
Baked	155	1 medium
Canned	120	½ cup
Tomatoes		
Raw	30	1 medium
Cooked or canned	25	½ cup
Tomato Juice	25	"
Turnips, cooked	20	"
Turnip greens	20	"

FRUITS

Apples, raw .... 70....1 medium
Apple Juice .... 60....½ cup
Applesauce
   Sweetened .... 90.... "
   Unsweetened .... 50.... "
Apricots
   Raw .... 55....3
   Canned, water pack.. 45....½ cup
   Canned, syrup pack..110.... "
   Dried, cooked,
     unsweetened ....120.... "
   Frozen, sweetened ...125.... "
Avocados ....185....½ 10-oz. size
Bananas, raw .... 85....1 medium
Berries
   Blackberries, raw..... 40....½ cup
   Blueberries, raw .... 45.... "
   Raspberries, raw ...... 35.... "
     Frozen, sweetened 120.... "
   Strawberries, raw ...... 30.... "
     Frozen, sweetened 120.... "
Cantaloupe, raw ...... 40....½ melon,
                   5" dia.
Cherries
   Raw .... 30....½ cup
   Canned red, sour,
     pitted .... 55.... "
Cranberry Sauce,
   sweetened .... 30....1 tbsp.
Cranberry Juice
   Cocktail .... 70....½ cup
Dates .... 250.... "
Figs
   Raw .... 90....3 small
   Canned, heavy syrup..110....½ cup
   Dried .... 60....1 large
Fruit Cocktail,
   canned in syrup.......100....½ cup
Grapefruit
   Raw .... 50....½ medium
   Canned water pack .. 35....½ cup
   Canned syrup pack.... 80.... "
Grapefruit Juice
   Unsweetened .... 50.... "
   Sweetened .... 65.... "
Grapes .... 45....3½ oz.
Grape Juice, bottled .... 75....½ cup
Honeydew Melon .... 50....2" x 7" wedge
Lemon Juice .... 30....½ cup
                  5....1 tbsp.
Lemonade .... 65....½ cup
Oranges, raw .... 70....1 orange
Orange Juice .... 60....½ cup
Peaches
   Raw .... 35....1 medium
   Canned, water pack .. 40....½ cup
   Canned, syrup pack ..100.... "
   Dried, cooked,
     unsweetened ....110.... "
   Frozen, sweetened ...105.... "

Pears
   Raw .... 100....1 pear
   Canned in heavy
     syrup .... 100....½ cup
Pineapple
   Raw .... 35....½ cup, diced
   Canned, syrup pack..100....½ cup or
                   2 slices
Pineapple Juice .... 60....½ cup
Plums
   Raw .... 30....1 plum
   Canned syrup pack ... 90....½ cup
Prunes, dried cooked
   Unsweetened ....150....9 prunes
   Sweetened ....260.... "
Prune Juice, canned.... 85....½ cup
Raisins, dried .... 230.... "
Rhubarb, cooked,
   sweetened ....190.... "
Tangerine, raw .... 40....1 medium
Tangerine Juice,
   canned .... 50....½ cup
Watermelon, raw .... 120....4" x 8" wedge

BREADS AND CEREALS

Cracked wheat .... 60....slice
Raisin .... 60.... "
Rye .... 55.... "
White .... 60.... "
Whole Wheat .... 55.... "

Other Baked Goods
Baking Powder Biscuit .130....each
Graham Crackers .... 55....2 medium
Saltines .... 35....2
Soda Crackers .... 45....2
Plain Muffins .... 135....each
Bran Muffins .... 125.... "
Corn Muffins .... 155.... "
Pancakes, wheat .... 60....4" dia.
Buckwheat Cakes .... 45.... "
Pizza (cheese) .... 180....⅛, 14" pie
Pretzels .... 20....5 sticks
Plain Pan Rolls .... 115....each
Hard Round Rolls ......160.... "
Sweet Pan Rolls ....135.... "
Rye Wafers .... 45....2
Waffles .... 240....4½" x 5½"

Cereals and Other Grain Products

Bran Flakes (40% bran)	85	1 oz.
Corn, puffed, presweetened	110	''
Corn and Soy Shreds	100	''
Corn Flakes	110	''
Corn Grits, cooked	90	¾ cup
Farina, cooked	80	''
Macaroni, cooked	115	''
Macaroni and Cheese	240	½ cup
Noodles, cooked	150	¾ cup
Oat Cereal	115	1 ounce
Oatmeal, cooked	110	¾ cup
Rice, cooked	150	''
Rice Flakes	115	1 cup
Rice, Puffed	55	''
Spaghetti, cooked	115	¾ cup
Spaghetti with Meat Sauce	215	''
Spaghetti in Tomato Sauce, with Cheese	160	''
Wheat, Puffed	100	1 oz.
Wheat, Puffed, presweetened	105	''
Wheat, Rolled, cooked	130	¾ cup
Wheat, Shredded, plain	100	1 oz.
Wheat Flakes	100	¾ cup
Wheat Flours		
Whole wheat	300	''
All-purpose flour	300	¾ cup sifted
Wheat germ	185	¾ cup

FATS, OILS, AND RELATED PRODUCTS

Margarine	100	1 tbsp.
Cooking Fats		
Vegetable	110	''
Lard	135	''
Salad or Cooking Oils	125	''

Salad Dressings

French	60	1 tbsp.
Blue Cheese, French	90	''
Home-cooked, boiled	30	''
Low-calorie	15	''
Mayonnaise		
Home-cooked	110	''
Commercial	60	''
Thousand Island	75	''

CANDY, SYRUPS, JAMS, JELLY

Caramels	120	1 oz.
Chocolate Creams	110	''
Chocolate, Milk, sweetened	145	1-oz. bar
Chocolate, Milk, sweetened, with almonds	150	''
Chocolate Mints	110	1 oz.
Fudge, Chocolate	115	''
Gumdrops	95	''
Hard Candy	110	1 oz.
Jelly Beans	65	''
Marshmallows	90	''
Peanut Brittle	125	''
Chocolate Syrup	40	1 tbsp.
Honey	60	''
Molasses, Cane, light	50	''
Syrup, table blends	55	''
Jelly	50	''
Jam, Marmalade, Preserves	55	''
Sugar	15	1 tsp.

DESSERTS

Apple Betty	175	½ cup
Angel Food Cake	110	2" Sector
Butter Cake, plain	180	3" x 2" x 1½" slice, or
	130	cupcake
Chocolate Cake, with fudge icing	420	2" piece
Doughnut	135	each
Fruitcake, dark	105	2" x 2" x ½" slice
Gingerbread	180	''
Pound Cake	130	1" slice
Sponge Cake	115	2" piece
Cookies, plain	110	3" dia.
Cornstarch Pudding	140	½ cup
Custard, baked	140	''
Fig Bars, small	55	each
Fruit Ice	75	½ cup
Gelatin dessert, plain	80	''
Pies		
Apple	330	4" piece
Cherry	340	''
Custard	265	''
Lemon Meringue	300	''
Mince	340	''
Pumpkin	265	''
Prune Whip	100	½ cup
Rennet Dessert Pudding	125	''
Sherbet	120	''

BEVERAGES

Ginger Ale	80	8-oz. glass
Kola type	105	''
Low-calorie type	10	''
Postum	5	1 cup
Coffee or Tea	0	''
Beer, 4% alcohol	175	12 oz.
Whisky, gin, rum:		
100-proof	125	1½ oz.
90-proof	110	''
86-proof	105	''
80-proof	100	''
70-proof	85	''
Wines, table use	70	3 oz.
Sweet Wines	120	''

Theresa Mullen

INDEX & CALORIE COUNT OF RECIPES